GUARDIANS
OF THE
PLANET

**Developed in partnership
with ClientEarth**

PUBLISHING

ILLUSTRATED BY JONATHAN WOODWARD
WRITTEN BY CLIVE GIFFORD
EDITED BY FRANCES EVANS
DESIGNED BY ZOE BRADLEY AND BARBARA WARD
COVER DESIGNED BY ANGIE ALLISON
CONSULTANCY BY DAMARA STRONG

First edition for the United States and Canada published in 2020 by B.E.S. Publishing

First published in Great Britain in 2019 by Buster Books, an imprint of Michael O'Mara
Books Limited, 9 Lion Yard, Tremadoc Road, London SW4 7NQ

All inquiries should be addressed to:
Peterson's Publishing, LLC
4380 S. Syracuse Street, Suite 200
Denver, CO 80237-2624
www.petersonsbooks.com

ISBN: 978-1-4380-8908-9

Date of Manufacture: November 2020
Manufactured by: WKT Co., Ltd., Shenzhen, China

Printed in China
9 8 7 6 5 4 3 2 1

CONTENTS

FOREWORD BY BRIAN ENO

Scientists now think there may be at least 20 sextillion (20,000,000,000,000,000,000,000) planets something like ours in the Universe. However, despite centuries of human observation of the heavens, the particular planet that we live on seems to be the only place where there actually is life in this unthinkably vast Universe. All the dazzling variety that we know about—from amoebas to antelopes, from zorillas to zebras—appears to be unique to this single planet.

But the last few years have been challenging ones for our planet. You all know the story: there's a swamp of plastic in the oceans, air pollution is reaching higher and higher levels, and whole species are disappearing every day. Climate change is changing lives and habitats across the globe.

This growing crisis sometimes seems unstoppable, but there is some good news. We've seen some remarkable people standing up and taking action to save this beautiful Earth, and there are now millions of citizens of all ages putting their energy and time into trying to tame the crisis.

One of the most effective of these groups is the charity ClientEarth, a coalition of lawyers, scientists, researchers, and others who have decided to work for the planet. I've been involved with ClientEarth for more than ten years and have seen firsthand how it uses the power of law to bring about a lasting difference.

"Using the Power of Law" means, for example, helping governments write laws that will encourage better practices of land use, waste disposal, and energy production. It also means enforcing existing laws—often by taking to court governments or other organizations who are behaving irresponsibly. From tackling air pollution to protecting forests, oceans, and wildlife, the law is a powerful tool in the battle to protect our environment. You can think of the people who work at ClientEarth as legal Guardians of the Planet. And now, by reading this book, you can become a Guardian, too.

Becoming a Guardian of the Planet sounds daunting, but together we can meet the challenge. By joining with other Guardians—in your local school, your friends and family, or connecting with groups across the world—you have incredible power to make a difference.

The future of the planet is in all our hands. By taking just a few of the actions in this book, you will be part of creating a better world for everyone, now and in the future. I'm delighted to join together with you, fellow Guardians of the Planet, and make a stand to protect our wonderful wildlife, clean up the air, and make the changes that will ensure our planet and all the incredible forms of life on it thrive.

INTRODUCTION:
GUARDIANS OF THE PLANET

The Earth has existed for over 4.5 billion years. Despite being bombarded by asteroids, trampled underfoot by dinosaurs, and suffering planet-wide ice ages, it has endured and flourished. But now Earth is in trouble and Guardians of the Planet are needed…URGENTLY.

This book is packed with tips and projects to help make our planet greener, safer, and more sustainable. One person alone cannot save the planet. But there are hundreds of things you can do at home, at school, and in your local community that can make a HUGE difference.

By the time you turn the final page, you will have all the skills and knowledge you need to be a fully-fledged Guardian of the Planet. Spread the word and encourage family, friends, neighbors, and classmates to do their bit, too. If we work together, we can make a vital contribution and help to look after the incredible world that we call home.

WILDLIFE WARDEN

According to a 2019 United Nations report, one million animal and plant species are threatened with extinction due to loss of habitats, climate change, and pollution.

FRIEND OF THE FORESTS

Since 1990, over 500,000 square mi. of forest have been burned or chopped down—an area bigger than South Africa.

HOME HERO

Humans have created a wasteful world. The United States alone produces over 220 million tons of waste each year—the weight of 604 Empire State Buildings.

GUARDIAN OF GREEN ENERGY

Climate change is warming up the Earth and ice caps are shrinking. NASA estimates that 240 billion tons of ice is lost each year.

WHY DOES THE PLANET NEED YOUR HELP?

Some terrible things which occur on our planet, from major earthquakes to erupting volcanoes, occur naturally. But many problems have been caused by a booming human population, and Earth is struggling to cope. Here are the seven key areas that will be explored in this book, all of which are in need of Guardian action:

FOOD WASTE FIGHTER

Rising demand for food is threatening crucial cycles in nature. Millions of square miles of wild habitats have been lost already.

FRESHWATER FRIEND

More than one in nine people don't have access to clean water. Contaminated drinking water causes over 500,000 deaths a year.

KEEPER OF THE COASTS AND OCEANS

Our oceans are under threat from pollution. Plastic trash alone kills over 1 million sea birds and 100,000 sea mammals every year.

CONNECTED TOGETHER

Everything on Earth is connected. This means that what you do at home and in your neighborhood, both good and bad, can have a massive impact on the planet. Before you get going on saving the world, it's important to understand how life on Earth is connected in many different ways and how human actions have affected these delicate systems.

LONG-DISTANCE DAMAGE

Life across Earth relies on natural cycles and systems. Water, for example, evaporates into the air and is carried by air currents to other places, where it falls as rain or snow. If the water mixes with harmful substances it can fall as acid rain, damaging environments far away from where the original pollution occurred.

Rivers also flow into the planet's network of oceans. This can mean that objects discarded in one place end up a long way away. In 2017, scientists even found chunks of Styrofoam in the remote waters of the Arctic Ocean.

Ecosystem is the term used to describe a community of different living things and their home environment.

Ecology is the study of how living things interact with each other and their environment.

TRADING PLACES

In the past, people relied on goods made and farmed near to where they lived. Today, billions of items are transported around the world. As the human population has more than tripled in the last 70 years, so the demand for food, materials, and products has boomed. Demand in one area can have a huge environmental impact elsewhere. For example, when people in Europe use large amounts of paper, the need for new paper means that trees in other parts of the world, such as the Amazon rainforest, are cut down and forest habitats are lost.

FOOD WEBS

Living things are connected by their relationships within their ecosystem. Food chains show how energy passes between things in an ecosystem, beginning with a producer—a living thing that makes its own food, such as a plant. Other living things (known as "consumers") eat producers and may then be eaten themselves, forming a chain.

Most creatures eat more than one type of plant or animal, so chains overlap to create a food web. A change in the population of one thing can have a major impact on the web. Pesticides, for instance, not only kill vast numbers of insects but also reduce the chances of survival of insect-eating birds, frogs, and other larger creatures.

Secondary consumer

Primary consumer

Producer

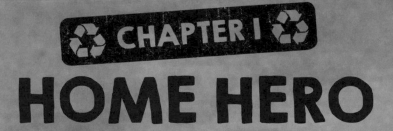

CHAPTER 1

HOME HERO

There's no place like home, but it's also one of the main places where stuff is wasted. This makes your home the perfect place to get started and begin your Guardian training.

WASTE AROUND THE WORLD

People living in wealthy, developed nations consume and throw away an awful lot. Each person in the US, for example, throws out an average of 4 pounds of trash per day. That means a family of five throws out 3.5 tons of trash a year. People in other parts of the world waste less. In Colombia, the figure is 2 pounds per day, while in Ghana it's just 3 ounces.

WHAT A WASTE!

Waste is a really good name for trash as it represents the waste of resources that were originally used to make the objects. Waste also uses resources when it's disposed of, including thousands of garbage trucks worldwide. Combined, they burn millions of gallons of polluting fuels each year.

14

By 2025, the World Bank estimates that humans will be producing 6.6 million tons of waste per day. To clean this up, we'd need a line of garbage trucks 3,100 mi. in length. That's as long as the country of China is wide.

WHERE DOES IT ALL GO?

Most waste is either burned or buried.

♻ Burning occurs in machines called incinerators. It can reduce the space that waste takes up by 90%. However, polluting gases, including sulphur dioxide and nitrous oxide, and toxic chemicals may all enter the air as a result.

♻ Thousands of tons of waste are illegally dumped. This can harm wildlife and it costs a fortune to clean up.

♻ Millions of tons of waste are buried in giant holes called landfills. There are half a million of these in Europe alone. Toxic chemicals in many landfills cause soil and water pollution. Greenhouse gases such as methane are also released as the trash decays.

15

TRASH TALK

It's time for GUARDIAN ACTION.
Your first job as a Home Hero is to spread
the word. If any of your family or friends
don't think waste is that big an issue,
hit them with the following facts.

BURYING THE PROBLEM

Pollution from landfills can travel long
distances, affecting soil and poisoning
rivers, streams, and underground
water supplies. Flammable gases and
chemicals also frequently catch fire,
starting landfill fires. There are more
than 8,000 fires every year at
landfill sites in the US alone.

WASTING AWAY?

Trash doesn't necessarily
decay quickly and easily.
While paper towels may take
just a month to biodegrade,
leather can take 50 years,
aluminum cans 100 years or
more, and plastic bottles
400 to 500 years.

LIFE AMONG GARBAGE

Garbage dumps in poorer, developing countries are growing and invading space taken up by local communities. Thousands of children live and play among broken glass, jagged metal, and toxic chemicals. Thousands more are forced to scour the garbage dumps to find waste items to sell.

THE COST OF WASTE

By 2025, the cost of dealing with rising waste around the world is expected to reach $375,000 million each year. That's money that could be spent building hundreds of hospitals or thousands of schools.

A LOAD OF TRASH

In 2016, humans produced 5.5 million tons of solid waste per day. If nothing changes, this figure is expected to more than double to 12 million tons of waste per day by 2100.

REDUCE, REUSE, RECYCLE

Can we all waste less? The simple answer is YES! But it will take a lot of effort on everyone's part—and that's where you come in.

THE THREE Rs

This diagram is called the waste pyramid and shows the ways to deal with waste, starting with the best at the top down to the worst at the bottom. Its key stages—known as the three Rs—are an essential part of your Guardian training.

REDUCE

This will get you an A+ in Home Heroism. The best way to tackle waste is to use fewer things, and to avoid using some things altogether.

REUSE

Reusing something is a good Guardian way of behaving. You are not consuming extra resources and you're keeping an item out of a landfill.

RECYCLE

This is a great way to help the planet, but it's not perfect. Although recycling saves resources, it also uses energy.

DISPOSE

As a Home Hero, your mission is to reduce waste as much as possible. Only throw something away if you're sure it cannot be reused or recycled.

JUST SAY NO!

The best course of action is to reduce how much new waste you create. It can be tempting to want to get your hands on the latest thing, but ask yourself some questions before you splash your cash…

Could I repair what we have at home or use something else instead?

Do I really need it?

Will I want it and use it three months from now?

Can I get it secondhand?

Could I borrow it from someone—I only need it for a short time?

USE AGAIN… AND AGAIN, AND AGAIN

You can also reduce your waste by buying items that last longer or can be repaired, and replacing items only when *absolutely* necessary.

♻ Billions of regular batteries become waste after they use up their charge. Rechargeable batteries can be recharged up to 1,000 times.

♻ Use washable cloths rather than disposable wipes or tissues.

♻ Printer ink and toner cartridges can often be refilled rather than thrown away.

♻ Pick a phone that has a replaceable battery rather than a sealed one.

♻ If your old laptop is slow, get a technician to spruce up its software. Upgrading one part, such as its memory, will cost and waste far less than replacing the whole machine.

♻ Pick up some more reuse ideas over the next few pages!

REPAIR AND REPURPOSE

Before your waste hits the garbage can, ask yourself the BIG question: can it be reused in some way or repaired? Finding creative ways to revamp your trash is not only good for the planet—it can be fun, too. Here are some handy ideas to get you started.

OPEN A REPAIR CAFÉ

In the past, people "made do and mended" rather than buying new—so why not revive some of these skills? Repair Cafés have become popular since they started in the Netherlands in 2009. People get together to fix clothes, bikes, computers, and other items, as well as learn and share skills. You can look at the Repair Café website to see if there is one near you. Or you could set up your own version with some friends, snacks, and an invited guest—an adult handyperson who's skilled at fixing certain things and can show you how.

Christmas and birthdays can be incredibly wasteful times of year. Open presents carefully so you can reuse the wrapping paper another time. You could also make your own gift tags from old greeting cards.

SEW EASY

It's tempting to throw away clothing because it's ripped or needs alterations. But remember that many clothing repairs are quick and easy with a bit of know-how, and can save money.

- ♻ Missing buttons or broken snaps can be replaced.

- ♻ A torn seam in your favorite T-shirt can be sewn up easily.

- ♻ Outgrown pants may have enough cloth in the hem to be made longer.

- ♻ Why not cover a small tear or stain with a badge or patch?

- ♻ Ripped jeans can be converted into shorts.

REPURPOSING AND UPCYCLING

Repurposing is when you reuse an object for a different task. Jars, for instance, make handy storage for craft materials and empty lip balm pots can make great containers for travel toiletries. You could also try "upcycling" to turn old, unwanted objects into new, cool items.

- ♻ Paint or decorate old cereal boxes, then cut out the top third of the narrow side to make a perfect paper or magazine holder.

- ♻ Potato chip bags can take over 80 years to decompose. Save up a load, turn them inside out, and wipe clean—then use them to create foil paper chains for a party.

- ♻ Paint empty coffee cans in bright colors so they can be used as plant pots to spruce up the yard or windowsill.

If you can't find a use for something, donate, don't discard! You may not be able to reuse an object, but that doesn't mean someone else can't. Check your local area for organizations that take items such as clothing, shoes, bikes, computers, and phones.

SECONDHAND AND SWAPS

Think secondhand stores are uncool? Think again! Get down to your local thrift store to bag some one-of-a-kind bargains and give the planet a helping hand, too.

CONSERVING RESOURCES

Buying people's unwanted goods is a great Home Hero way to shop. The items on sale have already used up resources. It takes 2,700 quarts of water, for example, to grow the cotton needed for one T-shirt. That doesn't include the energy used in its manufacture, or the fuel needed to take it to the store. Why consume more resources buying new, when you can enjoy something already made and keep it out of landfill?

If you've got lots of unwanted clothes and toys, try organizing your own thrift sale. You could raise money for a local environmental or wildlife charity.

TWO-WAY STREET

Another benefit of shopping secondhand is where your money goes. Instead of adding to the profits of a massive company, your cash goes to charity. Keep the process going by donating your own unwanted items to thrift stores and sales.

All money goes to charity

SWAP TILL YOU DROP

Another way to reduce consumption, yet refresh your wardrobe, is to hold a swap meet at school. This could be limited to clothes or it could be themed, such as book or video game swaps. Appoint an adult as a referee to stop any arguments and let everyone view all the items before swapping begins.

RECYCLING ONLINE

Freecycle is an organization made up of over 5,000 groups worldwide. Each group lists items people are offering for free, to stop them going to landfill or incinerators. You can sign up on its website and advertise your own goods to give away, but check with your parents first.

You can get real bargains in secondhand stores, including trendy clothing, rare books, and one-off toys and games.

For Sale

RECYCLING

Sometimes you can't find a new use for something or pass it on to a thrift store. That's where recycling comes in. Recycling is all about collecting and using waste to make something new. It reduces the waste sent to landfills or incinerators and saves many natural resources.

SERIOUS SAVINGS

Although recycling is pretty amazing, it's not perfect, which is why it's not top of the waste pyramid (see page 18). It needs lots of organization and effort to collect materials. Transporting, sorting, and processing the waste into new materials also uses energy.

Recycling, though, tends to use less energy and produce less pollution than making materials from scratch. Recycled aluminum, for example, takes just 5% of the energy needed to produce new aluminum. It's a similar story with plastic. Most plastic is made out of oil. Recycling a single ton of it can save 2,600 quarts of oil, thousands of kilowatt-hours of energy, and prevent over 1.5 tons of carbon emissions.

Glass doesn't biodegrade, but it can be recycled again and again. In 2017, the European Union recycled over 25 billion glass containers. That's 49 items for every member of its population.

RECYCLING RATES

Despite all the benefits that recycling can bring, vast amounts of items that could be recycled are not. Germany is top of the tree when it comes to recycling—around 60% of its solid waste was recycled in 2017. But other countries lag behind. The US only recycles just over a third of its waste, Greece and Israel less than one-fifth, and Mexico just 5%. Wherever you're from, one thing is certain—we could all recycle more to help the planet.

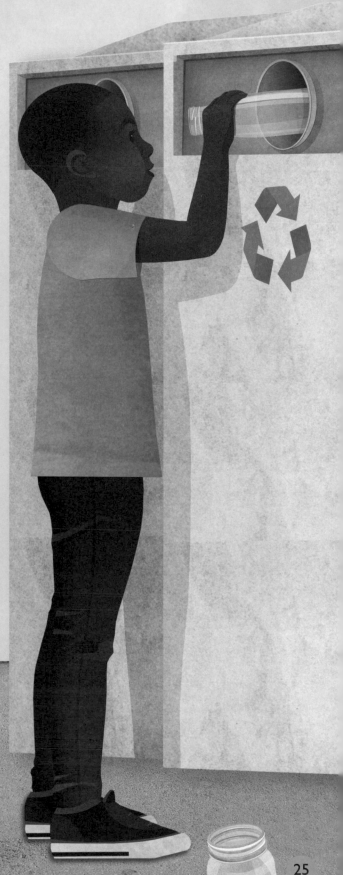

The energy saved from recycling one glass bottle will operate a 100-watt light bulb for four hours.

Recycling steel cans saves between 60% and 74% of the energy used to produce new steel.

For every 6 tons of glass that is recycled, 1 ton less of carbon dioxide (a key gas in global warming) enters the atmosphere.

YOUR RECYCLING MISSION

To really earn your Home Hero stripes, take charge of recycling around the house and at school. Here are some simple ways to whip your kitchen and classroom into shape.

TRASH DOS AND DON'TS

Your town or city probably offers curbside recycling of some materials already. If you're not sure what can be recycled at home, check online or visit the library to find out where recycling centers are and what they take.

Put recycling boxes next to your kitchen garbage can. Clearly color-code the boxes for different materials.

Make a recycling calendar to highlight the days when trash is picked up.

All sorts of plastic bottles, from salad dressing to shampoo, can be recycled. Rinse them out before you do.

Store items that can be recycled at a center but not in your bins, such as old keys, saucepans, and other cookware. They can then be taken to the center in one trip, avoiding multiple car journeys.

Cotton balls, broken mirrors, and toothpaste tubes CANNOT be recycled, so don't put them in your recycling bin. Items that contain a coating of wax or plastic, such as chip bags, cat food pouches, or paper coffee cups, can't be recycled either.

If you have a garden, consider composting food waste.

Sort glass into clear, green, and brown glass ready for the recycling center.

CLASS WAR ON WASTE

Recycling doesn't stop at home. Here are three ways to take your Guardian skills to school:

1. Have a class vs. class competition to see who can recycle the most in a month, with a prize for the winning class.

Recycling one aluminum can saves enough energy to run a TV for two hours!

2. Install more recycling bins in kid-friendly places. At each one, ask a class to produce an eye-catching display with inspiring recycling facts.

3. Organize a design competition to decorate the recycling bins. A regular swing bin, for example, can become a one-eyed monster just using paint, card, and old paper plates for the eyes. Even if you don't have a competition, making your bins fun and funky with a monster, robot, or nature design may help to encourage more recycling.

CHAPTER 2

GUARDIAN OF GREEN ENERGY

We use energy to build, heat, cool, and light buildings, and to eat, travel, and entertain ourselves. But meeting everyone's energy needs comes at a cost to the environment. The issues include air and water pollution, using up resources at a rate they cannot be replaced, and—the BIG ONE—climate change. Guardian of Green Energy, your planet needs you!

CLIMATE CHANGE

Earth is hotting up. NASA has measured how the planet's average surface temperature is more than 2°F higher than it was a century ago. And the rise is continuing. Seventeen of the eighteen warmest years ever recorded have occurred since 2001, and temperatures are predicted to increase by 2100. If nothing is done, this will have devastating effects.

- Changing weather patterns may lead to heavy rainfall and increased flooding, as well as droughts. This could damage ecosystems and crops and lead to food shortages.

- Ice caps at the poles, plus glaciers all over the world, will continue to melt.

- Sea levels will continue to rise, destroying wetlands and coastal communities and putting some low-lying islands totally underwater.

- More living things are expected to die out as the conditions become too harsh for them to adapt.

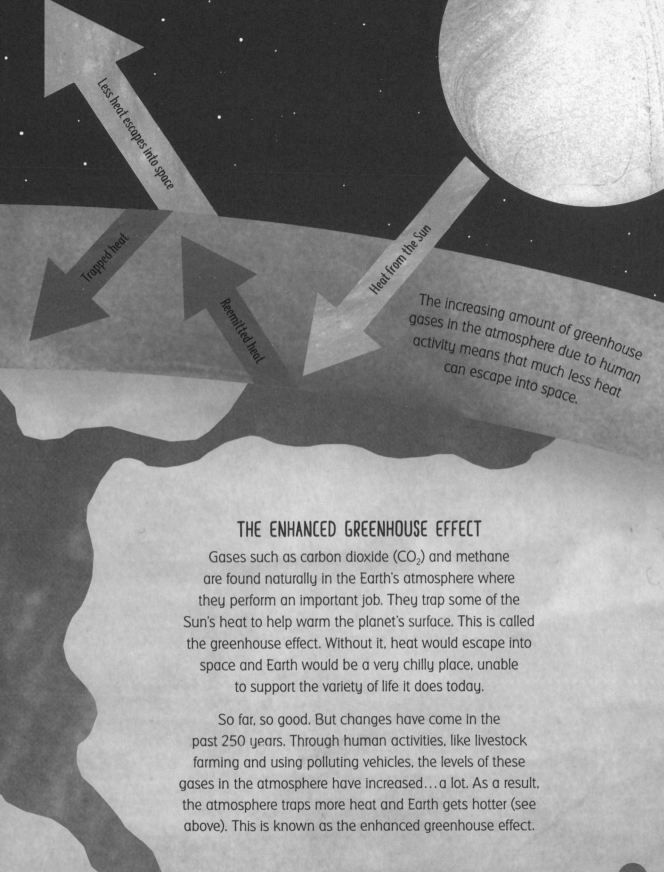

Less heat escapes into space

Trapped heat

Reemitted heat

Heat from the Sun

The increasing amount of greenhouse gases in the atmosphere due to human activity means that much less heat can escape into space.

THE ENHANCED GREENHOUSE EFFECT

Gases such as carbon dioxide (CO_2) and methane are found naturally in the Earth's atmosphere where they perform an important job. They trap some of the Sun's heat to help warm the planet's surface. This is called the greenhouse effect. Without it, heat would escape into space and Earth would be a very chilly place, unable to support the variety of life it does today.

So far, so good. But changes have come in the past 250 years. Through human activities, like livestock farming and using polluting vehicles, the levels of these gases in the atmosphere have increased…a lot. As a result, the atmosphere traps more heat and Earth gets hotter (see above). This is known as the enhanced greenhouse effect.

GREENHOUSE GASES

So, which gases are most responsible for the enhanced greenhouse effect, and what activities send them up into the atmosphere?

CARBON DIOXIDE

ALSO KNOWN AS CO_2

We pump 40 billion tons of this gas into the atmosphere every year, and some stays there for centuries. It accounts for three-quarters of the warming caused by humans. Burning fossil fuels, deforestation, and cement production are some of the biggest causes of CO_2.

WATER VAPOR

ALSO KNOWN AS H_2O

Water droplets in the atmosphere occur naturally as part of the water cycle and play a part in the normal greenhouse effect. The warmer the Earth's surface, the more water evaporates and turns into vapor, increasing the amount in the atmosphere.

NITROUS OXIDE

ALSO KNOWN AS N_2O

This gas stays in the atmosphere for around 110 years and contributes almost a tenth of all the warming that is happening as a result of human activity. Causes include farming, chemical fertilizers, burning fossil fuels, vehicles, and deforestation.

METHANE

ALSO KNOWN AS CH_4

This heat-trapping gas remains in the atmosphere for around ten years and is behind about one-seventh of the warming created by humans. The biggest causes include making and using fossil fuels, farming, and landfills.

THE ULTIMATE CARBON CULPRIT

Coal, oil, and natural gas are known as fossil fuels because they're created from the remains of animals and plants that lived millions of years ago. Fossil fuels contain carbon and can all be burned, releasing a lot of heat but also hefty emissions of greenhouse gases. Fossil fuels generate almost two-thirds of the world's electricity and power nearly all of the world's vehicles.

WHAT'S BEING DONE?

Many countries have signed agreements to reduce their emissions of greenhouse gases. Your first job as a Guardian of Green Energy is to get online to sign petitions and support campaigns to lower emissions. You can also do your bit by following the tips in the rest of this chapter to cut down your household's energy use.

Burning 1 ton of coal can produce more than twice its weight in CO_2 emissions.

Every person has an average carbon footprint of around 5 tons of CO_2 per year. That's an elephant's weight in planet-warming greenhouse gas.

IT'S ELECTRIC!

Each time you send a text or play a video game, you're using the world's most versatile form of energy—electricity. One hundred and fifty years ago, electricity was little more than a scientific curiosity. Today, every part of human life relies on it.

YOUR FLEXIBLE FRIEND

Electricity has many advantages. It can travel along cables from power stations to homes, schools, and offices. It can be converted into other forms of energy such as heat, light, and sound. And it can be controlled instantly with a switch. That also means you can switch items off and save energy REALLY easily!

CLEAN OR NOT?

Electricity does not produce direct carbon emissions. However, it isn't as clean as it seems. Many of the ways it is made create emissions or other forms of environmental impact. Check out which fuels were used to generate the world's electricity, according to the International Energy Agency's 2017 report:

39.3%	Coal
22.9%	Natural gas
16.0%	Hydroelectric power
10.6%	Nuclear
7.1%	Renewable energies and burning waste
4.1%	Oil

This means about TWO-THIRDS of all electricity is created by burning fossil fuels (oil, coal, and gas) that send huge amounts of emissions into the atmosphere.

Electricity is mostly produced at power stations by devices called generators, which are often powered by burning fossil fuels.

The amount of electricity used by people throughout the world has more than doubled since 1992.

CLEAN AND GREEN?

Even renewable energies, which we normally think of as emitting no greenhouse gases, are not all equally clean. Biomass is plant or animal matter that's sometimes burned to produce energy. It is often considered a renewable, but when you burn it in power stations, it releases even more emissions than burning coal.

MEASURING ELECTRICITY

How much electricity an object needs in order to work (its power rating) is measured in watts (W). Electricity use is measured in kilowatt-hours (kWh). This measurement is not as complex as it sounds—it just means 1,000 watts used for one hour. To measure how much electricity an object uses, multiply its power rating by the number of hours it is switched on. Then divide by 1,000 to get the kilowatt-hours. Use the power ratings below to work out how much energy some of these common electrical items use in your home. This will help you to work out where savings can be made.

- Iron   1,000–1,800 W
- Toaster   800–1,500 W
- Electric kettle   2,200–3,000 W
- Refrigerator   200–400 W
- LCD TV   125–200 W
- Games console   45–190 W
- Desktop computer   80–150 W
- Internet router   7–10 W
- Smartphone (being charged)   2.5–5 W

(Power ratings according to the Center for Sustainable Energy)

REMARKABLE RENEWABLES

Renewable energies are natural sources of energy that do not get used up like fossil fuels and have less environmental impact. Some of the energy in your home might already come from renewable sources, as they are becoming increasingly important. For example, more than 70 times the amount of electricity was generated by wind power in 2017 than in 1997.

WHAT'S UP WITH WAVES?

The power of the ocean's tides and waves can be used to create electricity. Companies have found it hard to build machines that can harness wave energy in large amounts, but there are some successful tidal power schemes. The Sihwa Lake Tidal Power Station in South Korea is the world's largest. It can produce up to 254 million watts of electricity.

Some tidal electricity generating systems use turbines, while others are turned by the flowing waters of the tide going in or out.

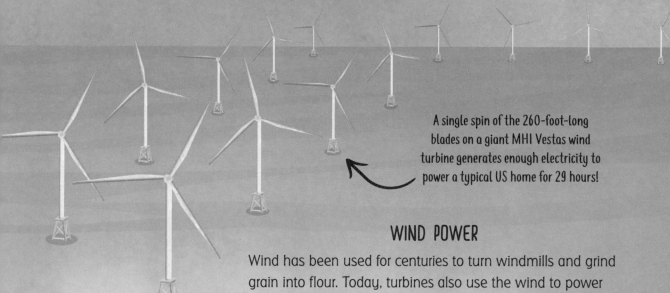

A single spin of the 260-foot-long blades on a giant MHI Vestas wind turbine generates enough electricity to power a typical US home for 29 hours!

WIND POWER

Wind has been used for centuries to turn windmills and grind grain into flour. Today, turbines also use the wind to power generators. Large wind farms can produce enough electricity to run 300,000 homes. In 2017, Denmark produced 43% of its energy using wind power, saving vast amounts of resources and reducing air pollution. However, because winds die down, turbines can't guarantee power around the clock.

ENERGY FROM THE EARTH

The "geothermal" energy in hot underground rocks can be used to warm buildings or power generators. Cold water is pumped into a system of underground pipes to absorb heat and send hot water or steam back to the surface. Iceland has lots of hot rocks underground, so nearly 90% of its homes are heated by geothermal energy. However, only some countries have enough geothermal energy that can be used easily.

SUPER SOLAR

Energy from the Sun can also be harnessed
in several ways to heat homes, create
electricity, and even to cook food.

USING SUNLIGHT

In some isolated communities in hot countries,
sunlight is used to dry out food to preserve it or may
be used to power a solar oven for cooking. Some
homes may also use the Sun's energy to heat water
in pipes without burning oil or coal or using electricity.

You can buy portable panels or
solar-powered backpacks to charge
phones and tablets on the move.

POWERFUL PANELS

Solar panels contain electronic circuits that
convert sunlight into electricity. A 10-square-foot
solar panel can produce 150–200 watts of power
without creating any pollution and can last 25
years. Over 1.8 million homes and businesses
in Australia use solar panels. The only problem
is that the panels need plenty of sunlight to
operate well.

MAKE A SOLAR OVEN

Warm up food in your own solar oven to see the power that renewables can unleash firsthand.

1. Make three cuts along the lid of a shoe box, 1 in. in from the edge, to form a flap. Cover the inside of the flap and box with aluminum foil, keeping the foil smooth.

2. Tape a sheet of black card where your food will sit. This will absorb heat and help to cook your snack.

3. Cover the opening in the lid (made by cutting out the flap) with two or three layers of plastic wrap. This lets sunlight into the box but traps the heat inside.

4. Prop the flap open with a stick. Place your oven in direct sunlight on a sunny day for at least 30 minutes to preheat.

5. After 30 minutes, open the lid (the part with the plastic wrap on) and place your food inside. A slice of cold pizza or marshmallows work well. Close the lid, prop the flap open again with the stick and wait. Check every 10–15 minutes until your food is warm.

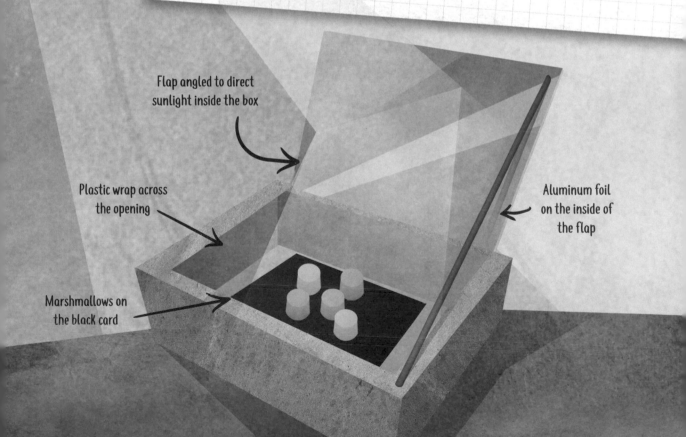

Flap angled to direct sunlight inside the box

Plastic wrap across the opening

Aluminum foil on the inside of the flap

Marshmallows on the black card

37

AIR POLLUTION

Clean air is vital for creatures to breathe, including people. Some air pollution occurs due to natural causes, such as dust and gases sent into the atmosphere by volcanoes. Most, though, is caused by humans, particularly through industry and vehicles. Here are some of the most common and dangerous substances.

SULPHUR DIOXIDE

When fossil fuels are burned in power stations that contain sulphur, this combines with oxygen to form sulphur dioxide (SO_2). Breathing in too much SO_2 can affect how your lungs work.

CARBON MONOXIDE

Carbon monoxide (CO) has no color or smell, but can be deadly. Breathing in lots of it can stop your blood carrying healthy levels of oxygen around your body. Carbon monoxide is produced by vehicles, stoves, and boilers that burn fossil fuels.

PARTICULATE MATTER

These tiny solid or liquid particles are usually less than one-ten thousandth of an inch in size. They include dust, soot, and chemicals from industry. They're small enough to be breathed in and can lead to asthma attacks and lung disease.

According to the World Health Organization, the health impact of air pollution is equivalent to 4.2 million deaths each year.

SMOG

The word "smog" was first used to describe a mix of fog and smoke produced by burning coal. It settled over some cities, causing great harm. Over 4,000 people died during the Great Smog of 1952 in London. Today, most smog is created when sunlight reacts with nitrogen oxides and other chemicals. The particles in smog can create a haze over a city, cause eye irritation, inflame lungs, and contribute to serious health problems, such as asthma.

Some cities try to combat smog by having car-free days. There's also a World Car Free Day every September—why not get your parents involved?

ACID RAIN

Rain, snow, or fog can be polluted by acid pollution in the atmosphere. Carried by winds, acid rain can fall great distances from where it was created, killing trees and harming freshwater environments and the creatures that live in them.

TRANSPORT TROUBLE

Back in 1900, there were no aircraft, few buses, and only a handful of cars. Today, there are over one billion vehicles on the world's roads and more than 100,000 flights carrying passengers every day. This has a major impact on the planet.

EXHAUST-ING

Most cars are powered by gasoline, a fossil fuel made from oil. Cars burn fuel and air in their engines' cylinders to produce power. The waste gases created leave the cars through their exhaust systems. A device called a catalytic converter removes some harmful gases, but all gas-powered cars still emit pollution and carbon dioxide. Diesel vehicles can be among the most polluting.

Airplanes burn up around five million barrels of oil as fuel every day, contributing to about 3% of all carbon emissions.

ADDITIONAL IMPACT

Cars, trucks, and motorcycles impact on the environment in other, indirect ways.

- Building a vehicle uses a lot of materials and energy. This includes all the energy used to make the materials that go into the car, as well as the power needed by machines to build it.

- Vehicle accidents kill an estimated 1.25 million people each year. Many millions more animals are also killed by collisions with vehicles.

- At the end of its life, a car can still cause harm. Much of a car can be recycled, but plastic, battery acid, and other materials need to be disposed of correctly or they can harm the environment.

- Millions of miles of roads circle the planet. They cut through land once occupied by wild plants, trees, and creatures.

GOING ELECTRIC

In 2018, the number of electric cars and buses on the world's roads passed four million. Producing electric cars still uses a lot of energy. The electricity they need to run may also have been generated by burning fossil fuels. However, they still tend to produce less carbon overall than regular cars. Most importantly, they produce no harmful air pollution as they run.

Walking and cycling are great Guardian ways of travelling as they are carbon-free!

OUT AND ABOUT

Some vehicle journeys cannot be avoided, but there's plenty you can do as a Guardian of Green Energy to reduce your family's reliance on gas-guzzling cars and vehicles. Here are some easy tips to consider when you're on the move.

2. When you're out and about, be a super Guardian of the Planet and pick up any litter you spot.

1. Many people make short car journeys when they could walk or cycle instead. Short car journeys are the most energy inefficient as the engine does not warm up and consumes more fuel as a result. In contrast, walking is a green and superhealthy way of getting from place to place.

3. Why not organize a walking school bus? Get adults to walk at the front and back of a line of kids to and from school.

4. To ensure you don't get lost on an unfamiliar walk, take a photo of a map of your journey before setting off. This is more energy efficient than using GPS on your phone and saves using up data.

5. International Walk To School Day is held every October. Check out the official website for ideas and events in your area.

COOL POOLING

Arrange car pools among friends and family so that when a car is used, it is full of people. Use a whiteboard for everyone in your house to mark up when they need to make trips.

Take the bus or train! Different modes of public transport may use gas, diesel, biofuels, or electricity, but they carry more people for every gallon of fuel used.

BIKE BASICS

Cycling is a fantastic way to travel. It's fast, fun, and energy efficient… but you must look after your bike. Get an adult to adjust your brakes and check that the height of your seat and handlebars is correct. Pump up your tires to help you to cycle quickly and smoothly. Use cycle lanes where you can, always wear a helmet, and follow all traffic signs and lights.

A basket attached to the front or back of your bike allows you to carry lots of stuff with ease. You can volunteer for small shopping trips on your bike to save an adult making a car journey.

ENERGY USE AT HOME

Learning about how energy is used at home and about new developments in energy efficiency can help you make some serious savings.

A WORLD OF DIFFERENCE

Home energy use varies greatly across the globe. Houses tend to be of different sizes and built in different ways, with some being more energy efficient than others. The number of appliances using energy in a home may also vary greatly.

ELECTRICITY USE PER PERSON A YEAR*:

Canada	15,546 kWh
Japan	7,820 kWh
European Union	5,908 kWh
Mexico	2,090 kWh
Indonesia	812 kWh

*According to the World Bank

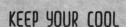

KEEP YOUR COOL

In some warm countries, a huge amount of energy is used on cooling homes with fans and air conditioning. In the US in 2017, cooling used 15.4% of all home electricity. That's a cool 212.5 billion kWh… or more than all the electricity used in the whole of South Africa by homes and industry in a whole year!

Turn down the air-conditioning, especially at night, wear cooler clothes, and close bedroom curtains in the day to stop your room from heating up.

When the heating or air-conditioning is on, always shut outside doors and windows. This stops heat or cool air leaking out and using more energy than necessary.

THE TWO-DEGREE CHALLENGE

Your next mission is to convince your family to take the "Two-Degree Challenge." This involves turning down the central heating by a couple of degrees. At first, you might need to wear an extra layer—or maybe try it out on milder days. Despite some likely moaning at the start, many households get used to a lower temperature really quickly. And the environmental benefits are BIG. Lowering the temperature on a thermostat in a room by just 2°F can stop 340 kg of CO_2 entering the atmosphere each year.

MON TUE WED THU FRI **SAT** SUN

ROOM TEMP **66**°F

‹ › ⌃ ⌄

Talk to your parents about installing a smart thermostat to only heat or cool your home when it really needs it.

ENERGY SAVING

There are opportunities everywhere for a Guardian of Green Energy like yourself to do your bit to save the planet. Here are a variety of ideas to help you reduce electricity and other energy use at home and away.

CFL lights use 60–80% less energy than incandescent bulbs. LED lights can use up to 90% less energy.

A GUARDIAN GUIDE TO ENERGY SAVING OUT AND ABOUT

- Check that the doors of fridges and freezers in food stores are all closed as you walk down the aisles. Mind your and other people's fingers as you do.

- If you're at someone's house, ask if they want a light on in an unused room, and if they're happy for you to do so, switch it off. It might influence them to turn more lights off in future.

- On vacation in a hotel? Tell your family to not demand fresh towels every day but only when they truly need a wash—this can save a lot of energy.

- Unless you need to reach the top of a 40-floor skyscraper, use the stairs rather than an elevator and encourage others to do so—it's also great exercise!

- Staying somewhere with a drafty door? Use rolled-up clothing or a spare blanket to block the gap at the bottom and stop precious heat escaping.

A GUARDIAN GUIDE TO ENERGY SAVING AT HOME

Encourage your parents to buy electrical products that use less energy than average. In the US, for example, many energy-efficient products carry an "Energy Star" sticker. In Europe, the EU energy label shows how energy efficient an object is.

Be a light saver. Switch off all unused lights when you leave a room.

Take a stand against standby. Switch off and unplug electrical items so that they don't consume power when not in use.

Remember, lots of energy is used to make materials in the first place. Buying less and reusing or recycling more materials is a big energy saver.

Use a clothes line rather than an electric tumble dryer.

Make sure phone and other chargers are unplugged when not in use.

If you spot Mom or Dad eyeing up a leaf blower in a store, convince them to save money and stick with a good old-fashioned rake—you could volunteer to rake the leaves yourself!

When cooking with your parents, put lids on saucepans of boiling water to save energy and make sure they're only boiling the amount of water they need.

Take shorter showers rather than baths, and run less water when you do hit the tub. This saves water as well as lots of energy used to heat it.

Let your hair dry naturally rather than using a hairdryer.

47

CHAPTER 3
FOOD WASTE FIGHTER

The saying goes that "you are what you eat." One thing's for certain—whatever you eat, your diet has some effect on the planet. Some foods and ways of farming, though, have a greater impact than others.

LOTS OF LAND

Land may seem endless, but it covers less than 30% of the planet. About a tenth of this is made up of icy glaciers and another fifth, such as mountaintops and deserts, cannot support crops. Of all the land that remains, half is used for farming.

More than three times as much land is used for farm animals as for growing crops.

Cows, sheep, and other farm animals create almost 15% of all the climate-changing gases generated by human activity (see page 30).

48

INTENSIVE FARMING

People's demand for food has seen farming change. Intensive farming uses giant fields and lots of chemicals to produce greater amounts of crops. As a result, woods and meadows, which once divided fields and provided homes for wildlife, have been destroyed, reducing biodiversity.

POISONOUS PESTICIDES

Pesticides are chemicals sprayed on crops that kill weeds or on insects that eat crops. Many of the poisonous substances they contain remain in the soil or are washed into rivers. These chemicals can build up in food chains (see page 13), harming lots of different animals.

A 2019 study by Greenpeace found 100 different pesticides in small rivers and canals across Europe.

NATURAL HELPERS

Organic farmers use methods with less environmental impact, such as encouraging ladybugs in their fields to eat pests instead of using pesticides. They may also sow "companion" plants beside their fields, such as mustard, whose bright flowers attract insects away from crops. Organic farming creates less pollution but smaller harvests, so the food is often more expensive.

FOOD FOR THOUGHT

Even though mountains of food are produced, technically enough to feed everyone, people go hungry every day. Much food is wasted and food consumption is not spread evenly around the world.

WORLD HUNGER

People in wealthy countries have so much food that their biggest health problems often come from overeating and obesity. Yet millions of people, usually in poorer countries, face a daily battle to get enough food to survive.

Hunger is not the feeling you get when you miss an occasional meal—it is a desperate lack of food that your body needs to stay healthy. According to the World Food Program, 795 million people—twice the population of the US—are undernourished. This means they do not get enough nutrients for their body to grow or be able to fight off diseases. This leads to some horrifying statistics.

Around 21,000 people die each day from starvation or hunger-related diseases.

As many as 201.3 million children under five—more than twice the population of Germany—suffer from poor growth or health issues because they have not received enough food.

Undernutrition causes the deaths of 3.1 million children each year.

HUNGER AND CLIMATE CHANGE

Many people who struggle to get enough food live in areas of the world that are particularly vulnerable to extreme weather events, such as droughts or flooding. Natural disasters are often made worse by climate change; when they occur more frequently, it becomes harder for farmers to recover and so food shortages increase.

A FAIRER FOOD SYSTEM

Your plate of food may contain items from the other side of the world. While this gives you incredible choice, transporting food around uses up fossil fuels and creates greenhouse gas emissions. At the same time, buying food from sustainable sources abroad can provide a vital income for farmers in poorer countries. Here are some tips to help make your dinner eco-friendly as well as ethical:

- Read about the causes of global hunger online. Support petitions calling for fairer deals for small-scale farmers around the world.

- When you buy exotic products, such as tea, chocolate, and bananas, buy Fairtrade to support farmers in developing countries.

- Buy organic food from local farms and other sources when it is in season. Look online to see what's in season in your country.

- Eat more meat-free meals and follow the tips in this chapter to make sure less food goes to waste.

- Have a go at growing your own fruits and vegetables—which involves next-to-no food miles! Turn the page for some tips.

GROW
YOUR OWN

You may not be allowed to turn your lawn into a farm or have a garden of your own, but you can still be a green-fingered Guardian. Growing even a tiny amount of your own food can be rewarding and a lot of fun.

START WITH A SEED

Ask family members or neighbors who garden about what grows best in your area. Plants such as radishes, tomatoes, chives, and salad greens all tend to be quick growers.

Follow the packet's instructions. Sew the seeds in trays and keep them watered as the directions suggest. Once they have sprouted and grown strong, you can plant them in pots. Use old flowerpots or yogurt containers rather than buying new containers. You can even make your own pots out of newspaper (see page 63).

GARDENING WITHOUT A GARDEN

If you don't have much space but want to give gardening a try, why not try creating a windowsill garden with trays of pots, or using small shelves on your balcony?

An old canvas shoe organizer can also be turned into a great herb or salad garden. Fill each pocket with compost and healthy seedlings. Get an adult to attach a hook to the wall that can take the weight of your soil and plant-filled hanging garden.

If you're really stuck for space, you can create a mini herb garden in the individual compartments of an old egg carton.

A GUARDIAN GUIDE TO GROWING ORGANIC

To gain true Food Waste Fighter status, try to grow your plants as organically as possible. That could mean using your own homemade compost and avoiding chemical pesticides or fertilizers. Here are some ideas to get you started.

- Spray aphids with water and nothing else, and put crushed eggshells around the base of your plants to ward off slugs.

- Remove weeds by hand rather than spraying them with pesticides.

- To stop fungus growing on your plants, mix several teaspoons of baking soda with warm water, pour into an old spray bottle, and squirt on to the plants. The baking soda makes it harder for the fungus to grow and it should start to disappear.

- Most insect pests don't like strong flavors, so prepare a stinky spray to ward them off. Mince a clove of garlic and half an onion and add to a quart of water. Leave for 30 minutes, then add a teaspoon of cayenne pepper and two teaspoons of liquid soap. Spray over plants to protect them.

COMPOSTING

Composting involves collecting plant and food waste and leaving it to rot. It is nature's way of recycling materials into something useful, as compost is packed with nutrients that can improve a garden's soil. And it's easy.

BIG BENEFITS

Composting disposes of most plant and food waste—from fruit and vegetables, to cereal crops and grass clippings—in a natural, harmless fashion. It does not generate the large emissions of methane that buried landfill does and can be performed at home, on farms, and in schools with little special equipment.

In a regular compost bin, it takes about a month for the materials to start breaking down and usually six months to a year for mature compost to form. The compost can be spread over soil where its nutrients, such as nitrogen and potassium, help plants to grow.

Straw, cardboard, torn-up newspaper, and crushed-up eggshells can also be composted.

BE A COMPOST CHAMPION

If you have a garden, build your own composter and use the compost it makes to add nutrients to your flowerbeds. If you don't have a garden, you could suggest composting as a project at school. You'll need a large container to place all the food and other waste in. Many towns and cities also offer free compost bins.

Composting works best when the conditions inside the bin are warm and damp, so pick a sunny but sheltered spot. Open-bottomed bins can be placed directly on top of soil. If your composter has a base, put a layer of soil at the bottom. Microbes and worms in the soil help to speed up the composting process.

NOT FOR COMPOSTING

Don't put anything in your compost that contains plastic or plasticlike materials, as these don't break down. Other things to avoid are:

- Pet poop and droppings
- Meat scraps or bones
- Dairy products, including butter and cheese
- Fish skins
- Foil, plastic, or metal items
- Glossy paper and magazines
- Coffee pods
- Plants that were sprayed with harmful chemicals
- Tea bags, unless the bags are made of cotton or hemp

In the US, over 23 million tons of mown grass and food waste are composted every year.

GO VEGGIE

Vegetarians are people who do not eat anything involving the death of creatures, including foods or ingredients made from animal parts such as gelatine. Vegans consume no animal products whatsoever—so no cheese, animal milk, or honey. Even if turning totally veggie isn't for you, you can still make a difference by eating less meat.

MEAT NO MORE

People give up eating animal products for a number of reasons, including their religious faith or concerns about animal welfare. Many turn veggie or eat less meat because of how its production affects the environment.

Some 56 billion animals are killed for meat every year. While alive, they use up a huge amount of the Earth's resources. According to *The American Journal of Clinical Nutrition*, a typical American meat eater's diet requires 17 times more land, 14 times more water, and 10 times more energy than a vegetarian's.

The amount of calories in the food eaten by the world's cattle could feed up to 8.7 billion people—more than the world's human population. Around 75% of all soy grown, for instance, is used to feed livestock, a crop which could be turned into food for people.

It takes more water to produce meat than it does vegetables. Around 287 quarts are needed to produce 2 lbs. of potatoes, but 15,400 quarts to produce 2 lbs. of beef.

A 2018 Oxford University study found that 83% of all farming land is used for rearing animals. Yet, they produce only 18% of all the world's food calories eaten by people.

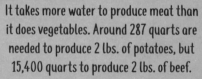

TRY IT OUT

Veggie food can be just as exciting, nutritious, and varied as meaty meals. You probably eat some meat-free meals already—whether it be a tasty margherita pizza or a baked potato. Here are some further ideas for how you can reduce your meat consumption and enjoy some tasty, healthy meals:

- Ask your parents to try some meat-free alternatives, such as vegetable burgers or tofu.

- Organize meat-free Mondays where you and your family go veggie for the day.

- Large portobello mushrooms, grilled or roasted with slices of beet, tomato, and cheese can make a delicious hot sandwich.

- Take meat-free lunches to school, replacing the ham in a sandwich with cheese, or taking falafels wrapped in pita bread.

- Swap pieces of chicken or pork for mushrooms, zucchini chunks, and cashew nuts in a stir-fried noodle dish.

IN THE GARBAGE

It's not just what you eat that matters. Every time you throw out an overripe melon or a brown banana, you are playing a tiny part in a surprisingly BIG issue. The Food and Agriculture Organization of the United Nations estimates that a third of all food produced in the world for people is never eaten. This enormous loss is equal to more than 3.5 million tons of food every day of the year.

As much as ten times more food is wasted per person in developed nations than in the developing world. The food wasted in Europe alone could feed as many as 200 million people. And there are additional wasted resources, as all this uneaten food has to be disposed of in some way. In the UK, 18 million tons of waste food—the weight of 54 Empire State Buildings—is thrown into landfills.

SO, WHAT FOODS ARE WASTED AND NEVER EATEN EVERY DAY OF THE YEAR?

45% of all fruit and veg

35% of all fish and seafood

HUNGRY FOR CHANGE?

A good way to reduce waste is to think of food as you would any other product (remember the "waste pyramid" on page 18?). The best course of action is to not overbuy or cook too much. Storing food well, such as putting cereals and cookies in airtight containers, keeps them fresh for longer.

LEFTOVERS

Using excess food from an earlier meal is a great Guardian way to eat. You have already used ingredients, time, and energy when making a meal, so it's smart thinking to reuse these foods and turn them into something equally delicious. Set yourself the challenge of taking part in a leftovers meal once a week with your family. There are some ideas down the side of this page to get you started.

Old potatoes can be mashed up, then fried with chopped onions, sliced cabbage, and herbs to make delicious potato cakes.

Not-quite-fresh bread can be grilled with tomato puree, veggies, and cheese to make an easy pizza.

Overripe bananas can be peeled, placed inside freezer bags, and frozen to be used at a later date for nutritious smoothies.

30% of cereal crops, such as wheat and corn

20% of meat

20% of dairy products

PACKAGING PROBLEMS

You're well on your way in the fight against food waste, but waste doesn't end with the stuff you don't eat. It often surrounds the food you purchase in the form of packaging.

FOOD PACKAGING

Millions of pounds of food packaging becomes waste each year. In the European Union in 2015, an average of 365 lbs. of packaging waste—the weight of two men—was generated per person. Much of this is food packaging, from plastic trays to tea bags sealed in foil and housed inside a cardboard box.

Some packaging is necessary for handling and transporting food. Eggs carried by trucks, for example, would break without cartons. Packaging can also preserve food, keeping it fresh until it's used. Much packaging, though, is not vital and is often only there to make the product more attractive for customers to buy.

Market stalls and wholefood and health shops often sell many items loose. You can bring your own reusable container to store the bought food in to transport it home.

Reuse paper bags to carry loose fruit or vegetables and transport heavy vegetables, like potatoes, in a reusable canvas bag.

PICK YOUR PACKAGING

When faced with a choice at the supermarket, think before you buy. If packaging is unavoidable, see if it has a recyclable logo.

Recyclable logos vary but the most common version—known as the "Universal Recycling Symbol"—looks like this.

Certain foods are packaged in a mixture of materials, only some of which can be recycled. This cardboard tray, for instance, can be recycled but the single-use plastic jacket around it cannot.

BE A WASTE WARRIOR

Challenge yourself to reduce the amount of food packaging thrown away in your home in a week. Weigh the amount of food packaging—such as cans, bottles, boxes, and plastic containers—that was generated by your family in a regular week. Spend the next week cutting down on packaging, using the tips on this page to help. Weigh the packaging waste at the end of the second week to see how much you've saved—a quarter or more is great!

Drink water from the faucet rather than buying lots of bottles of plastic water.

Drink juice diluted with tap water rather than cans of soft drinks. One bottle of juice can provide many more drinks with much less packaging weight.

PLANET-FRIENDLY FOOD IDEAS

Your food waste training is almost complete. As you've seen, there's a lot that can be done to make enjoyable meals and reduce the impact they have on the planet. Here are a few fun ideas and projects for you to try.

Visit a vegan or vegetarian restaurant or food store. You can learn about the huge range of meat-free meals and maybe get inspiration for your own cooking.

Make a personalized plastic lunchbox rather than throwing away plastic and paper bags every day. You could stencil on your name or cover your box in stickers.

Helping your parents with a food shop? Take a "shelfie" photo of what's in the fridge before you leave. This means you can keep track of what's being bought and make sure nothing goes to waste.

Pack a metal fork in your lunchbox, too, so you never have to use disposable plastic ones.

Get your family to sign up to a vegetable box scheme and support local, organic farmers.

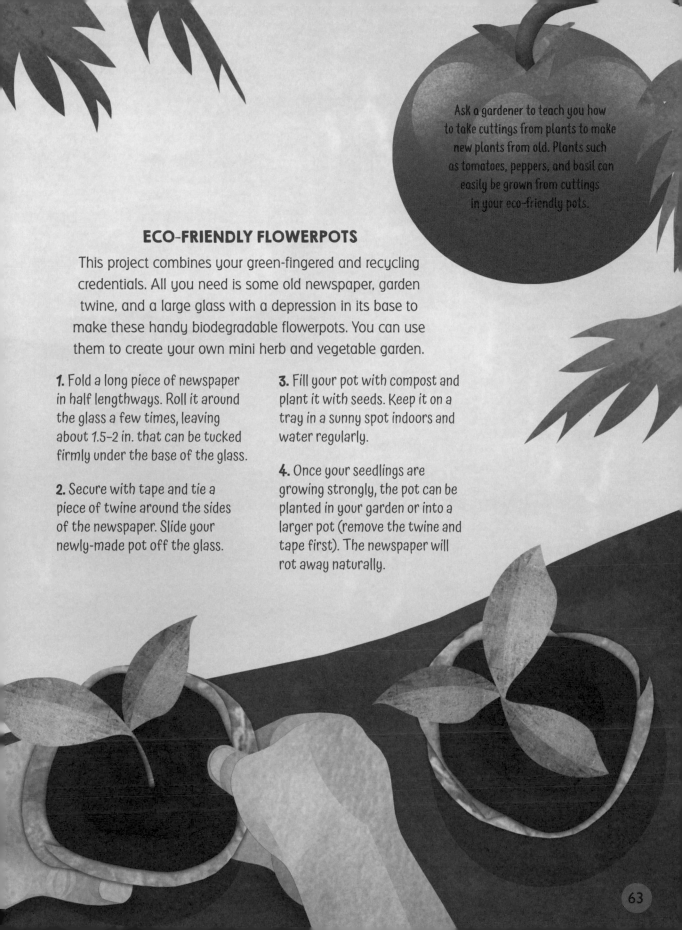

Ask a gardener to teach you how to take cuttings from plants to make new plants from old. Plants such as tomatoes, peppers, and basil can easily be grown from cuttings in your eco-friendly pots.

ECO-FRIENDLY FLOWERPOTS

This project combines your green-fingered and recycling credentials. All you need is some old newspaper, garden twine, and a large glass with a depression in its base to make these handy biodegradable flowerpots. You can use them to create your own mini herb and vegetable garden.

1. Fold a long piece of newspaper in half lengthways. Roll it around the glass a few times, leaving about 1.5–2 in. that can be tucked firmly under the base of the glass.

2. Secure with tape and tie a piece of twine around the sides of the newspaper. Slide your newly-made pot off the glass.

3. Fill your pot with compost and plant it with seeds. Keep it on a tray in a sunny spot indoors and water regularly.

4. Once your seedlings are growing strongly, the pot can be planted in your garden or into a larger pot (remove the twine and tape first). The newspaper will rot away naturally.

CHAPTER 4

FRESHWATER FRIEND

Water is not something you probably think about a lot. Just turn on the faucet and fresh, clean water usually flows out. But water isn't distributed equally around the planet. Pollution and water waste have made the problem worse and some supplies are at breaking point. Freshwater Friends are urgently required.

WHY IS WATER SO IMPORTANT?

You ideally need to drink 2 quarts of water a day to stay healthy. Water helps your body to control temperature, transport nutrients, flush out waste, and much, much more.

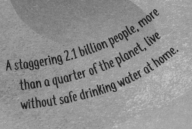
A staggering 2.1 billion people, more than a quarter of the planet, live without safe drinking water at home.

UNCLEAN AND UNFIT

People rely on water to farm and to keep themselves clean and healthy via sewage systems. Poor sewage systems can result in rivers, lakes, and wells becoming contaminated with human and animal waste or polluted by chemicals dumped by industry. Dirty water can also spread lethal diseases, such as cholera, dysentery, and polio.

Diarrhea caused by unclean water and poor sanitation is responsible for as many as 842,000 deaths a year, according to the World Health Organization.

IN SHORT SUPPLY

About three-tenths of Earth's fresh water lies underground. People access it by digging wells, but in some parts of the world these water sources are under stress: the water in over half of India's wells is being used up more quickly than it can be replaced.

Climate change also affects water supplies. For instance, more than a quarter of Peru's Quelccaya Ice Cap has melted since the 1980s. Further loss could deprive thousands of people living nearby of a drinking supply.

65

WASTING WATER

About 97.5% of the world's water is too salty for humans to use, meaning the fresh water from your kitchen faucet is really precious. But your family's water use is likely to mount up rapidly. These handy tips can help you to tackle the problem firsthand.

When washing fruit and vegetables, don't run them under a faucet. Fill a small bowl of water instead and wash them in that.

In the time it takes you to count to ten, a running kitchen faucet can send 1.5 quarts of clean water straight down the drain. Always use a plug when washing dishes!

In 2016, the Water Research Foundation estimated that a typical American used 235 quarts of water each day—just 31 people's annual water use would fill an Olympic-sized swimming pool.

CLEAN COSTS

Washing machines are marvelous things, but they can use lots of water: 3–7 quarts for every pound of clothes is typical. This can mean that a large washing machine consumes 160 quarts or more for a single load. So it's important to make each wash count.

● If your shirt or shorts are borderline wash-ready but don't smell to high heaven, use them to play sports and get an extra wear out of them before they go into the wash.

● Encourage your family to use the washing machine sparingly. They should only switch it on once a full load is ready to be washed.

● If a piece of clothing is basically clean but just has a small stain or mark on it, sponge it off with a little water poured into a cup.

● If your favorite shirt or skirt is dirty and you need it urgently, you can hand wash it using a small bowl of lukewarm water and a teaspoon of detergent.

Cooking vegetables in a steamer uses less water than boiling them. Baking foods in the oven uses even less!

Keep a jug of water in your fridge. This water will be chilled whenever you need it and saves you running a faucet until the water gets cold.

HOME TRUTHS

While cooking, washing dishes, and drinking water uses around 20% of all household water, the biggest offenders are found in the bathroom where almost 70% of a typical home's water is used. Cutting down the amount of water you use there is easy with a bit of know-how. Here are some simple ways to make bathtime more freshwater friendly.

FAUCETS

Turn faucets off tightly. A dripping faucet can waste 1 quart of water per hour—that's 8,760 quarts a year.

TEETH

Brushing your teeth with a faucet running fully uses as much as 12 quarts per minute. Turn the faucet off while brushing and fill a glass of water to rinse.

TEMPERATURE

When making the water cooler using a mixing faucet, turn the hot faucet down rather than the cold faucet up. This saves energy and water!

TUBS

Baths typically use 75–90 quarts of water. Take a shower instead—but read the tips on the next page before you do!

TOILET

Don't flush your toilet unless it's necessary. Many people don't flush their toilet after every use to save water.

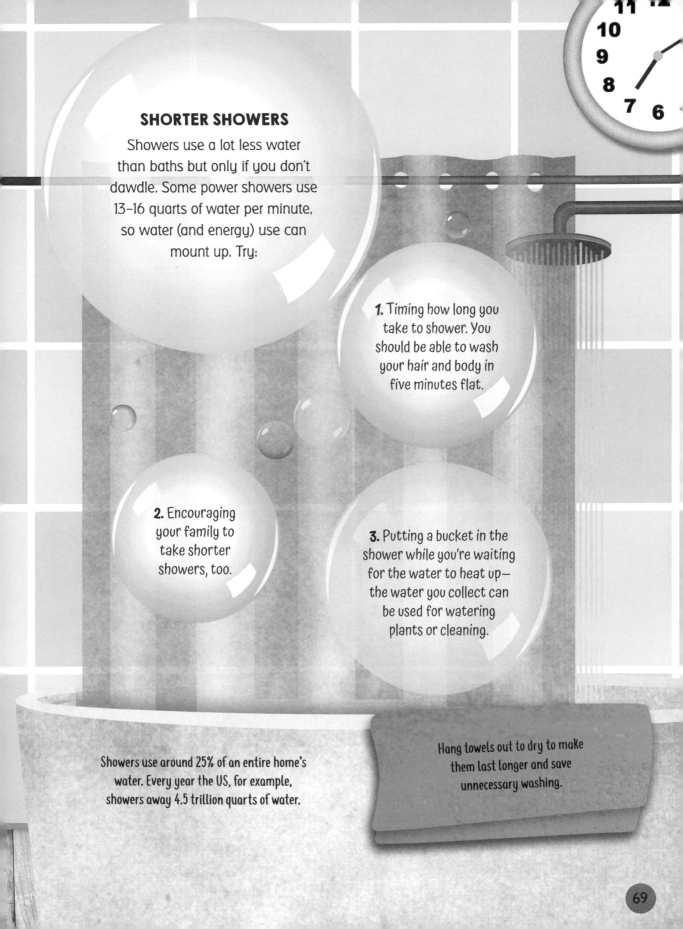

SHORTER SHOWERS

Showers use a lot less water than baths but only if you don't dawdle. Some power showers use 13–16 quarts of water per minute, so water (and energy) use can mount up. Try:

1. Timing how long you take to shower. You should be able to wash your hair and body in five minutes flat.

2. Encouraging your family to take shorter showers, too.

3. Putting a bucket in the shower while you're waiting for the water to heat up— the water you collect can be used for watering plants or cleaning.

Showers use around 25% of an entire home's water. Every year the US, for example, showers away 4.5 trillion quarts of water.

Hang towels out to dry to make them last longer and save unnecessary washing.

YOUR WATER FOOTPRINT

People often think of their impact on the environment in terms of their carbon footprint—how many greenhouse gas emissions their actions create. In a similar way, thinking about how much water your actions use can help you figure out how to make savings.

WATER, WATER EVERYWHERE

It's not just the water you drink or flush away; everything you consume used water in its production. The amounts required can be shocking. For instance, according to Friends of the Earth, around 160 baths' worth are needed to make just one smartphone.

H_2O TO GO

In the first six months of 2017, 1.77 billion quarts of bottled water were sold in the UK. The water inside is only part of the story. On average, it takes two to three times more water to make the bottle itself. A supereasy way to save water, and reduce the oil and energy used to make plastic, is to buy a reusable bottle and fill it for free from the faucet at home.

WATER CYCLE WONDERS

Water is recycled between the Earth's surface and atmosphere in the water cycle. During the cycle, water evaporates from the ground and the surface of bodies of water. It passes into the atmosphere as water vapor and falls back to Earth as rain, sleet, or snow. Bearing this in mind can help you to save a huge amount of water outdoors.

BUILD A BARREL

Rain can be channeled from roofs into water barrels or collectors and then used around the yard or to wash bikes and cars. You can easily make your own barrel by placing an old plastic garbage can under the downspout. Get an adult to drill a hole in the top for the downspout and add a spigot near the base.

If every home in France collected one water barrel's worth of water, a staggering 4,560,000,000 quarts of free, fresh water could be harvested.

When your yard needs a drink, use your collector to fill a watering can instead of using a hose or sprinklers. Sprinklers are big water wasters; even a small one can use 1,000 quarts of water per hour.

The hotter it is, the quicker water evaporates, so water plants in the morning or evening when temperatures are lower. This means less water evaporates and more sinks into the soil.

WATER POLLUTION

Saving water is only part of the story. Pollution can transform life-giving water into a harmful hazard. It can make the water of a lake, river, or well unsafe to drink, depriving local communities of their water supply and threatening them with diseases.

It's not all about people, either. According to *National Geographic*, over one-fifth of the 10,000 known species of freshwater fish have either become extinct or are threatened with extinction. Much of this is due to waters being polluted.

IN HOT WATER

Hot water may not seem like pollution but it heats up surrounding river or lake water (this is known as "thermal pollution"). This reduces how much oxygen the water can hold, killing fish that require certain oxygen levels to survive. Power stations and factories are the biggest culprits.

MINE TIME

The mining industry uses large amounts of water, and sometimes toxic chemicals, when extracting certain metals from their rocky ores. These often reach water supplies, either accidentally or through illegal dumping. This type of pollution is called acid mine drainage.

In 2018, the heavily polluted Bellandur Lake in India caught fire and blazed for 30 hours, sending ash over 5 mi. away.

FARM HARM

Chemical pesticides and fertilizers can run off into rivers and other water sources. They can kill wildlife or cause a major buildup of algae, which may choke the life out of a river or lake.

POOP-LLUTION

In many countries, toilet waste is carefully treated to remove harmful substances from the water supply. But in poorer and developing countries more than 80% of human waste is sent untreated into rivers, lakes, or the sea.

WHAT'S BEING DONE?

Cleanup campaigns can make a real difference. In 1957, the Thames River in London, UK, was so polluted it was declared biologically "dead." A cleanup campaign has resulted in the return of 125 different species of fish, as well as seals, today. In 2017, China launched 8,000 river and lake cleanup schemes, while other countries are banning the dumping of harmful substances.

CLEAN AND GREEN

Trying to rid a giant river or lake of all its pollutants may seem a hopeless task. But as a Freshwater Friend there are many things you can do to make a small, but crucial, difference.

DOWN THE DRAIN

Your kitchen or bathroom is a good place to start. Be careful with what you flush or wash down the sink. Sometimes people think that just because it's out of sight, it's disappeared, but that's simply not true. Sending pollutants into your wastewater system merely passes the problem on.

Oils, fats, and paints can clog pipes. Place them in a container and take it to your local recycling center when full.

In some countries, it is estimated that a third of all medicines bought at a drugstore or prescribed by a doctor never get taken. Never flush or pour them down the drain.

Your local sewage system is great at handling pee and poop, but it's not a giant wastebasket. Don't flush dental floss, Band-Aids, wet wipes, or tissues. Throw them in the garbage instead.

WHAT CAN YOU DO?

Some cleaning and cosmetic products contain substances which are harmful if they enter the water supply. Fortunately, many companies have produced eco-friendly alternatives, but it's also supereasy to make your own green and clean versions in some cases:

- Lemon juice makes an epic cleaner of windows when a squirt is added to some warm water. White vinegar mixed with water in a spray bottle also makes a great cleaner of surfaces and sinks.

- Did you know that baking soda is a natural stink absorber? A teaspoon in a small box at the back of your fridge can absorb funky smells. It can also tackle stinky sneakers. Just sprinkle some in the shoes, leave overnight, and clean out for fresh footwear.

- Mix a tablespoon of olive oil, a teaspoon of honey, and one egg yolk together really thoroughly and you have a natural hair conditioner. Apply, leave on for 30 minutes, and then rinse off.

- Instead of throwing away your tired bar of soap, recycle it. Grate it up, get an adult to help you bring a pan containing a few cupfuls of water to a boil and then switch the stove off. Add your grated soap bit by bit. Stir until it melts and is the consistency you want, and leave it to cool. Then pour into an old soap dispenser bottle and place next to the sink, ready to use.

HABITAT HARM

Littering and dumping can harm water sources just as much as pollution from factories. Acid from batteries dumped in rivers can leach out into the water. Discarded plastic, such as bags and fishing lines, can kill animals, while chewing gum can stick to fur or feathers, preventing the creature from staying clean.

CAN-TASTROPHE

Beverage cans dumped in rivers and ponds can injure animals and block waterways. Worse are the plastic rings that hold packs of cans together. While many are now made of biodegradable plastic, the process doesn't happen fast enough and the rings still kill large numbers of creatures. Birds and mammals may get strangled by or entangled in the rings, unable to eat or move.

TAKE ACTION

Many canals, rivers, and ponds get overgrown, polluted, and used as a dumping ground. Why not organize a cleanup of a local water source near you?

- Check out your cleanup site with an adult and take a pen and paper to list every problem. Make a map of the safe areas to work in.

- Wear tough shoes and clothing that covers your entire body and protects you from plants that may prick or sting.

- Wear thick gardening gloves as you pick up garbage. Watch out for broken glass and other objects that can injure you. Ask an adult to pick up anything sharp or dangerous.

- Trash pickers or fishing nets can be used to fish out garbage.

- Sort the garbage on-site into different materials and into color-coded containers or trash bags. That way, it can be easily taken to a recycling center.

- Ask an adult to help you to move larger objects, such as furniture, old bikes, and shopping carts.

- Remove weeds that are choking other plants or stopping the water from flowing. But be careful not to remove native plants or overhanging branches that provide shade.

- If the banks are bare, plant suitable grasses and shrubs. These help to bind the soil together and provide shade, as well as dropping seeds into the water for fish to eat.

- Take photos before and after your cleanup to show your school.

Celebrate World Water Day on March 22nd by organizing a cleanup. You can find lots of other activities on the official World Water Day website.

CHAPTER 5

KEEPER OF THE COASTS AND OCEANS

Oceans are awesome. They contain over 96% of the world's water and provide homes and food for billions of creatures. Oceans are also a vital part of the water cycle and help to control the climate and weather around the planet. Keepers are needed to protect these unique and delicate habitats.

Oceans are packed with life—from the most microscopic plankton to the blue whale, the largest creature ever to have lived on Earth.

The Census of Marine Life has identified about 250,000 species living in the oceans, but it's thought there are many, many more.

Tiny, single-celled organisms called phytoplankton, along with other marine plants, help to produce half of all the oxygen found in Earth's atmosphere.

Oceans absorb more than half of the heat that reaches Earth from the Sun. Their currents run for thousands of miles, distributing their warmth around the world.

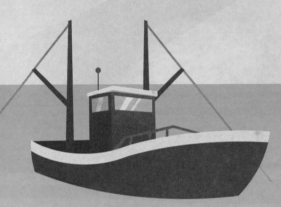

Around 90% of all the world's trade, goods, and raw materials are carried by ship.

Around 90 million tons of fish and seafood are hauled out of the oceans every year.

CO_2 dissolves in water, and oceans take up a large amount of CO_2 from the atmosphere. Without them, the pace of global warming would be much faster.

The sea is an important source of leisure and fun. Some island countries, such as the Maldives and the Bahamas, rely on seaside tourism for between one- to two-fifths of their entire income.

OCEAN POLLUTION

Oceans are beautiful places, but they have been used as watery garbage cans for centuries. When fewer people lived on Earth, the oceans could cope, but today's booming human numbers and large industries are having a serious impact.

PESTICIDES

According to the US National Ocean Service, four-fifths of the pollution that reaches the oceans comes from land. This includes large amounts of pesticides washed from farmland into rivers.

"DEAD ZONES"

In many parts of the world, human waste is piped straight into the sea. The sewage can create "dead zones"—areas of the ocean containing little or no oxygen, meaning that hardly any life can survive.

CHEMICALS

Some industries deposit waste directly into the sea. It may include dangerous chemicals such as lead, mercury, and various acids.

DRAIN DAMAGE

Other pollution that reaches the ocean includes vehicle oil and bleaches dumped down drains.

BIG BUILDUP

This diagram shows how pollution can affect ocean food chains:

1. Plankton in seawater absorb the polluting chemicals as they feed.

2. They are eaten in large quantities by small fish and other creatures. The poisonous pollutants build up in their bodies.

SICK SLICKS

Oil spills occur from ships, oil tanker accidents, leaking pipelines, and underwater oil wells. Many are small, but some can be large and deadly to wildlife.

- If oil is swallowed it can kill many types of sea creatures.

- Oil sticks birds' feathers together, preventing them from flying.

- Oil on fur and feathers stops their insulating power. The affected creatures often die of extreme cold.

- Oil floats and can block out sunlight, meaning that plankton and underwater plants can't make food.

- When it washes up on the coast, oil can contaminate more living things. It can also kill plant life whose roots bind the soil together. Without the plants, soil can be more easily eroded.

3. Larger predators, such as bigger fish and squid, eat the smaller fish and marine creatures. The poisonous chemicals can collect in their bodies faster than their bodies can break them down.

4. A large sea creature, such as a shark, can contain a concentration of these harmful chemicals several million times higher than those found in the waters in which they live.

THE PERILS OF PLASTIC

One of the biggest challenges facing a Keeper of the Coasts and Oceans is plastic. When plastics were invented, they were thought of as wonder materials. They were light, cheap to produce, and didn't break down quickly. But plastics have become a HUGE problem that's impacting our oceans hard.

DRASTIC PLASTIC

Studies in 2015 estimated that between 5.3 million and 14 million tons of plastic enter the oceans each year. If all 14 million tons were turned into milk cartons they would stretch over 26 million mi.—54 trips to the Moon and back.

Many plastic items, such as bags or disposable cups, are only used for a few minutes before being thrown away, yet take hundreds of years to biodegrade.

FLOATING GARBAGE DUMP

The world's biggest garbage dump floats in the Pacific Ocean between the Hawaiian Islands and the United States. The Great Pacific Garbage Patch is a giant, swirling area where plastics and other garbage are drawn together by an ocean current called a gyre. The Ocean Cleanup Foundation estimates it covers an area of 615,000 mi^2. That's more than three times the size of Spain.

PLASTIC POLLUTION

Plastics enter oceans in many ways—from being dumped in rivers to getting flushed down toilets. Scientific studies and TV documentaries such as *Blue Planet II* have highlighted this problem and its effects on wildlife.

- Creatures can get trapped in or strangled by plastic wires or lines.

- Plastic eventually breaks into small particles known as microplastics. These make their way into ocean food chains and are eaten by a range of creatures, including people. According to the Marine Conservation Society, the average European person who eats seafood also eats 11,000 plastic particles a year. Fine, plastic fibers can get sucked into fish's gills, too.

- Plastic bags, balloons, and other colorful items can be mistaken for food by marine creatures. In some cases, their stomachs become full of plastic, which they cannot digest, leaving them no room to process real food.

- Plastics can be carried long distances across an ocean, affecting marine life far away from where they entered the water. They can wash up on beaches, causing harm to life there as well.

A hungry sea turtle cannot tell the difference between a jellyfish and a plastic bag.

PLASTIC ATTACK

Plastics are posing an enormous problem for the world's oceans and Guardian action is needed. Here's what's currently being done, and how you can play your part.

NEW RULES

Some governments and companies have put schemes in place to reduce plastic use. In 2002, Bangladesh became the first country to ban lightweight plastic bags. Other countries, including Rwanda, China, and Morocco, have followed suit. Some nations encourage less use through taxing plastic bags or making them harder to obtain.

In the UK, a plastic bag tax was introduced in 2015. The sale of plastic bags has dropped by over 80% since.

In Kenya, anyone found using, making or selling plastic bags can face a fine of up to US$38,000 or four years in prison.

In 2018, Seattle became the first US city to ban plastic drinking straws and plastic cutlery.

In 2016, France announced a ban on all single-use plastic cups, plates, and cutlery to begin in 2020.

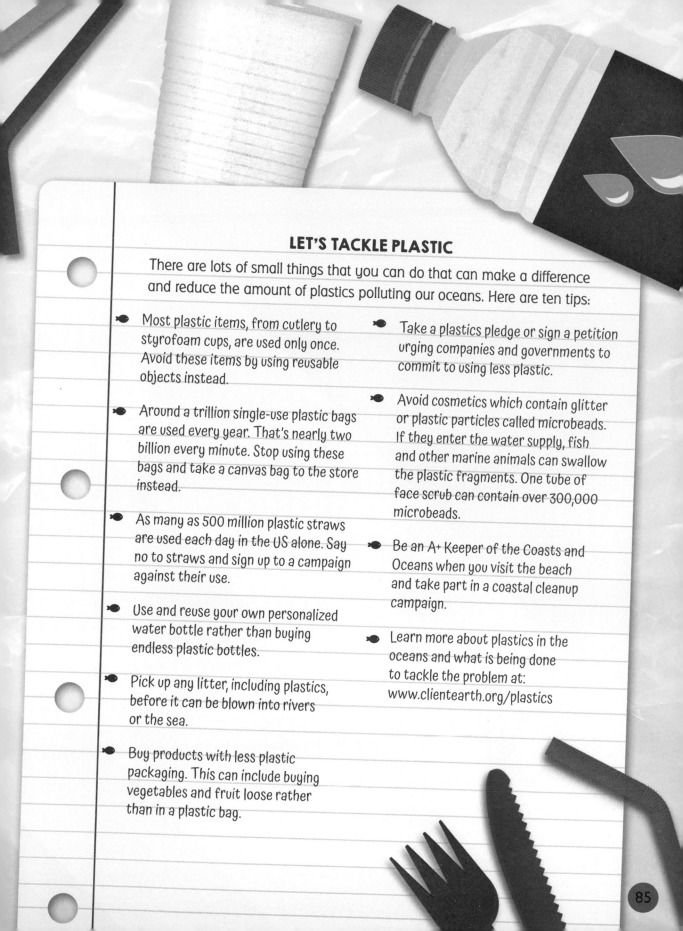

LET'S TACKLE PLASTIC

There are lots of small things that you can do that can make a difference and reduce the amount of plastics polluting our oceans. Here are ten tips:

- Most plastic items, from cutlery to styrofoam cups, are used only once. Avoid these items by using reusable objects instead.

- Around a trillion single-use plastic bags are used every year. That's nearly two billion every minute. Stop using these bags and take a canvas bag to the store instead.

- As many as 500 million plastic straws are used each day in the US alone. Say no to straws and sign up to a campaign against their use.

- Use and reuse your own personalized water bottle rather than buying endless plastic bottles.

- Pick up any litter, including plastics, before it can be blown into rivers or the sea.

- Buy products with less plastic packaging. This can include buying vegetables and fruit loose rather than in a plastic bag.

- Take a plastics pledge or sign a petition urging companies and governments to commit to using less plastic.

- Avoid cosmetics which contain glitter or plastic particles called microbeads. If they enter the water supply, fish and other marine animals can swallow the plastic fragments. One tube of face scrub can contain over 300,000 microbeads.

- Be an A+ Keeper of the Coasts and Oceans when you visit the beach and take part in a coastal cleanup campaign.

- Learn more about plastics in the oceans and what is being done to tackle the problem at: www.clientearth.org/plastics

FISHING FRENZY

Whether it's a tuna salad or fish sticks, millions of people eat fish every day. And why not? It's usually very nutritious and tasty. But an enormous rise in the demand for fish and other seafood has had devastating effects.

OVERFISHING

In the rush to meet demand, the world's giant fishing fleets have overfished many ocean areas. The remaining fish cannot reproduce quickly enough to make up the numbers. Overfishing puts great strain on the balance of life in the oceans. When numbers of one fish species dwindle, it can seriously affect other fish, seabirds, seals, and sharks which rely on it for food.

According to Greenpeace, 95% of all southern bluefin tuna and Pacific bluefin tuna fish have already been caught or killed.

Bottom trawling is a type of fishing using heavily weighted nets dragged along the sea floor. These can damage habitats, smash coral reefs, rip up ocean plants, and capture young fish unsuitable for eating.

NOT IN MY NET

The fishing industry uses the term "bycatch" for the unwanted fish and sea life caught accidentally. Bycatch can be as high as two-fifths of all of the fishing industry's catch. It's not just billions of fish. According to the World Wildlife Fund, the number of other creatures caught and killed as bycatch each year is shocking:

- 100 million sharks
- 250,000 or more leatherback and loggerhead sea turtles
- 300,000 or more dolphins, porpoises, and small whales
- Many thousands of seabirds

One way you can tackle this immediately is to look for canned fish that has been caught by pole and line or handline rather than in nets. This reduces the amount of other creatures snared as bycatch.

The nesting female population of Pacific leatherback turtles has dropped by 95% since 1980.

CORAL REEFS

Coral reefs only occupy 0.1% of the world's oceans, yet support more than a quarter of the world's marine life. Australia's Great Barrier Reef alone is home to 133 types of shark, 1,625 species of fish, and 3,000 species of mollusks (shellfish). However, reefs are delicate and vulnerable. If the corals disappear, so may the millions of creatures that live in them.

REEF GRIEF

According to the World Wildlife Fund, a quarter of all reefs are thought to be damaged beyond repair. Another two-thirds are believed to be under serious threat. Increasingly acidic seawaters caused by carbon emissions is one reason. Here are some others:

Dredging the seabed with machines can cause silt and sediment buildup to harm coral.

Some unscrupulous fishermen use explosives in the water to stun large numbers of fish and damage coral in the process. Others use poison to stun fish, which also harms the coral.

Tourists may trample on coral, break off pieces as souvenirs, or buy gifts made from local coral.

WHAT CAN YOU DO?

You may live a long way from the nearest coral reef, but there are still things you can do to help preserve and protect them.

- If swimming near coral, be careful not to knock or break any with your hands, feet, or flippers.

- Never buy coral products or souvenirs. You may think the damage is done but, when a piece of coral is sold, the seller is likely to restock.

- Do your part to combat climate change through energy conservation.

- Save water and reduce waste so there is less chance of pollution entering the oceans and contaminating reefs.

CORAL BLEACHING

Coral relies on nutrients obtained from zooxanthellae, tiny, plantlike things that live inside them. They are very sensitive to water temperature and a rise, via climate change or thermal pollution, can cause them to leave the coral. This results in coral losing its bright colors. Bleached coral can recover, but is very vulnerable and may die out.

A DAY AT THE BEACH

Trips to the beach or a walk along the coast can be fun.
But they can wreak havoc on the environment if you don't
act responsibly. As a Keeper of the Coasts and Oceans, follow
these suggestions to make sure your day out stays eco-friendly.

SUN-SCREAM

It's important to wear sunscreen to protect your skin
from the Sun's harmful rays. However, some sunscreens
contain chemicals that are harmful to sea life. Oxybenzone,
a chemical found in some spray-on sunscreens, can harm
coral even in small amounts. Avoid sunscreens that contain
oxybenzone, and also octinoxate and octocrylene.

Rub your sunscreen
in really well and don't
waste any in the water.

SPF
50

Don't bring meals to the beach
in plastic bags that can blow
away and cause harm.

COASTAL CLEANUP

If you live close to the coast, ask at your community center about cleanup events, or look up Ocean Conservancy, which runs the International Coastal Cleanup every year. Since it began over 30 years ago, more than 12 million people have volunteered and collected over 220 million lbs. of trash—the weight of 3,700 humpback whales!

Each day you're at the beach, take a short break and be a Keeper of the Coasts and Oceans. Spend half an hour combing part of the beach, picking up any litter you find (wearing gloves for safety).

Leave shells in rock pools where they are. Chances are there's a living creature inside!

Many sand dunes are held together by the plants that grow in them. Stick to paths to avoid damaging this delicate balance.

Don't disrupt the natural diets of coastal creatures by feeding them your food.

CHAPTER 6

FRIEND OF THE FORESTS

Trees are found on all continents except the icy wastes of Antarctica. They exist in many different environments, from hot, dry scrubland to icy Taiga forests in the Arctic Circle. Trees cover 30.8% of the land on Earth, yet many are under threat from disease, pollution, and human activity. These awesome giants need Friends of the Forests to look out for them.

TIMBERRRRR!

People rely on trees for food, firewood, medicines, paper, and other materials. These demands, along with trees being cleared to make way for farmland, means that we are losing forests at an alarming rate—as much as 27 football fields of forest every minute, according to the World Wildlife Fund. This deforestation is having a major impact on the planet.

TROPICAL RAINFORESTS

One of the most extraordinary types of forests are the warm, wet rainforests found near the Earth's equator. They are packed with more species than any other ecosystem on the planet. The Amazon is the world's largest rainforest, measuring more than twice the size of India. Scientists estimate it is home to over 390 billion trees, but much of it remains unexplored, and dozens of new species of plants and creatures are discovered there every year.

The three-toed sloth lives in the trees of the Amazon and spends most of its time hanging upside down from branches. It only climbs down about once a week to go to the bathroom.

THE KEY TO TREES

A tree's leaves are packed with special structures called chloroplasts. They allow a tree to make its own food via a chemical reaction called photosynthesis. Photosynthesis converts light from the Sun, water taken up by the tree's roots, and carbon dioxide absorbed from the air into food and oxygen.

Trees also absorb carbon dioxide as they grow. A large tree takes in around 50 lbs. of CO_2 every year.

TREE-MENDOUS!

Whether found in a giant forest or standing alone on your street, trees provide places with an outstanding range of benefits beyond absorbing carbon dioxide.

Trees provide vital habitats for large amounts of life. According to the UK Royal Parks, a single mature oak tree can be home to 500 species—from squirrels and starlings, to moths and mites.

The leaves, twigs, and fruits that fall from a tree form a carpet of material on the ground. This provides a home and food for snails, spiders, centipedes, and beetles. These are eaten by birds as well as frogs, rabbits, and other animals, creating an entire food web from the tree's lost parts.

Trunks provide homes for millions of minibeasts. The insects burrow into the bark and provide essential food for creatures as varied as woodpeckers, lizards, and tree shrews.

Tree roots can extend many feet, taking in water and nutrients from the soil. They also filter and store polluting chemicals from water in their roots, helping to protect the local environment.

The liquid sap that flows through trees can also be useful to people. Rubber trees, for example, produce a sap known as latex, used to make products such as balloons and doctors' gloves.

Trees produce vast quantities of food for people around the world. This ranges from the nuts of pecan, walnut, and pistachio trees, to the fruits of orange, peach, and cherry trees, not to mention spices such as cinnamon and nutmeg.

The shade cast by a tree attracts all sorts of critters, including humans. Scientists estimate that trees can cool an area by 2–6°F, through the water they evaporate and the shade they produce.

Roots also help to bind the soil together so that it does not blow or wash away. In rainy places where trees have been removed, soil erosion and mudslides can be a big problem.

TREE TASKS

As a Friend of the Forests, your BFFs are the trees in your neighborhood. Get to know them by mapping them out, examining each tree, and learning to identify the different species.

LEAF RUBBINGS

You can record a tree's bark pattern or leaf shape and texture by making a rubbing. Take a piece of plain (recycled) paper and place it on the bark. Use a colored crayon or soft pencil to rub quickly over the paper so that the bark's pattern appears on the sheet. Do the same with a leaf found on the ground by putting it on a hard surface and placing your paper over it.

There are a whopping 60,000 tree species in the world. Get a book from the library or use an online guide to identify the species that live in your local area.

BE A TREE DETECTIVE

Grab a large piece of paper and draw a simple map of your yard and local area. Head outside and take this map and a notebook with you. Number each tree you come across on the map so you know its location and try to perform as many of the following tasks as possible:

- What is the overall shape of the tree? Is it wide at the top or is it tall and narrow? Draw its outline to help you to identify it.

- Does it have smooth, ridged, or really rough bark? Feel the bark and, if you've time, take a bark rubbing.

- Does the tree have flowers, fruits, or nuts? Draw or describe them.

- What are its leaves shaped like? Don't pull a leaf off the tree. Instead, pick up one that has fallen to the ground to tape to your map or to make a rubbing.

- Look closely and write down any creatures you see using the tree for food or shelter.

- When you're home, use online guides or books to identify the trees you saw. Which species were the most popular in your area?

Dozens of schemes all over the world allow people to adopt a tree, to look after it, and help it to grow and flourish. Check online or at your local park to see how you can get involved.

97

TREES UNDER THREAT

You'd think something as amazing as a tree would be treasured. But every day tens of millions of trees are chopped down—a total of over 15 billion each year. Some are replaced, but not all. This means that many forests are shrinking in size ... and fast.

HOW AND WHY?

Trees are lost due to pollution, such as acid rain, as well as forest fires. However, one of the main causes of deforestation is the demand for wood, paper, and other products made from trees, such as palm oil. Forests are also destroyed to make way for farmland, towns, roads, or industrial sites.

Two-fifths of Pakistan's forests and a quarter of Nepal's forests have been destroyed since 1990.

Without tree roots to help bind it all together, soil can be blown or washed away, turning once fertile land into desert.

BIG IMPACT

As trees are so great for the environment, you can imagine how terrible losing so many can be for the planet. Deforestation results in more carbon dioxide reaching the atmosphere. Plants, creatures, and people who live in forests all lose their homes, while those that remain in the area may struggle to survive.

Orangutan numbers have plummeted by as much as half in the last 100 years and deforestation is the main cause.

Without trees blocking out some of the Sun's heat, the moist forest soil can dry out and other plants may find it hard to grow.

Brazil has lost one-fifth of its Amazon rainforest since 1970. That's an area more than twice the size of Germany.

BRING THEM BACK

It's not all bad news. Nations and organizations are trying to slow the rate of deforestation and some have planted new forests. According to the UN, both Vietnam and Cuba have over 55% more forests now than they did in 1990, while Uruguay has more than doubled its forests in the same time.

99

WOOD LIKE TO MEET

Take a trip to a local woods or forest and be prepared to be amazed. Compared to your local survey of your street's trees, you're about to enter a wooded wonderland!

VISIT TIPS

There's no better way to get up close and personal to nature than a forest visit. Many countries have protected areas of forests. In the United States, National Park Week in April sees free admission to the country's parks and protected area of forests.

- Don't litter and if you see anyone else's litter pick it up carefully and put it in the nearest litter bin. The forest thanks you!

- Stay on designated paths and trails so you don't trample on wild plants. Straying off course can get you lost and in trouble very quickly.

- Don't snap branches or pull off live leaves. If you want a souvenir of your visit, take a photo or make a rubbing of a leaf or bark.

- Or buy something at the park's gift shop—any money spent or donated there tends to go toward keeping the forest intact and healthy.

Keep March 21st in mind as the UN has declared it to be the International Day of Forests. There may be local events in your neighborhood parks, woodlands, or forests.

FOREST FIRES

Natural phenomena, like lightning, start some forest fires but many are caused by humans. A 2017 study using US Forest Service statistics found that 1.2 million US fires were caused by people. Some were started deliberately. Other common causes are bonfires getting out of control, campfires, and littering. Fires can spread rapidly, killing creatures and destroying vast numbers of trees. A fire in Portugal in 2017 killed as many as 30 million trees.

Never light a fire underneath trees or bushes. Campfires should always be built in open areas and kept small and supervised at all times.

If you notice an unsupervised or out-of-control fire, contact your local fire department.

PAPER SAVER

People use a PHENOMENAL amount of paper, often without thinking about it. This has a big impact on the environment as new paper is produced, mostly from trees, at a rapid rate.

Over four billion trees are used to make paper every year. That's around 40% of all trees cut down by industry and the number is rising.

PAPER COSTS

A typical person in the European Union uses around 350 lbs. of paper every year. Much of it is in the form of packaging, tissues, and toilet paper, as well as paper bags. A single, mature tree can make as many as 700 paper bags, which sounds a lot, but a busy supermarket can use them all up in an hour or less.

Most paper is produced using large amounts of energy and chemicals, too. In fact, it takes around 5–10 quarts of water to make one sheet of $8\frac{1}{2} \times 11$" paper, while the wood pulp and paper industry is thought to consume 4% of the world's energy use.

Recycling paper really saves the planet. Every 2,000 lbs. of paper recycled saves 17 adult trees, 26,500 quarts of water, 1,400 quarts of oil, and enough electricity to power an American home for about five months!

CUT DOWN ON PAPER

You probably already recycle some paper at home or at school, but be vigilant and try to recycle even more. There are also many things that you can do to reduce your paper consumption.

- View magazines online rather than buying paper copies.

- Buy books, notebooks, and toilet paper made from recycled paper.

- Use your local library when you want to read exciting new stories or learn new facts. You can even start your own mini library by swapping books between you and your friends.

- See if your printer at home or school can print on both sides of each sheet. You can make the font size smaller and the margins of the page wider, so a long document takes less pages to print.

- Convince your household to use a whiteboard to make notes and messages rather than scribbling them on paper.

- Get used to carrying a washable fabric handkerchief to reduce the amount of paper towels or tissues you use.

- If your home receives a lot of junk mail, ask your parents to look into canceling as much of it as possible.

- Cut up old paper into similar-sized sheets, hole punch them in one corner, and tie together with string to make a recycled notepad.

More than four times as much paper is produced today as was 40 years ago.

PLANT A TREE

What better way to help trees out than to plant new ones? If you don't have space at home for a new tree, campaign to plant trees at your school. Many schemes offer free or very cheap young trees for planting at schools and in neighborhoods.

THE HOLE STORY

Most trees are best planted in spring or fall and will need space in which to grow. Your tree may be small now, but think how big it will be in 20, 30, or 40 years!

Dig a hole as deep as the roots of your tree, but two to three times as wide. Handle the tree gently by its root ball, not by its thin trunk which could be damaged. Place it in the center of the hole and cover the roots with soil and compost. Water well. If your tree is over 3 feet tall, ask an adult to drive a stake into the ground and tie it to the trunk for extra support.

Young trees need care and attention. Make sure the tree is well watered for the first few years—but be careful not to over water it during rainy periods. Keep a circle around its base (about 3–5 ft. wide) free of weeds. You could also add a layer of mulch around the tree to give extra nutrients and keep water in the soil.

Before you plant anything, find out what sorts of trees are suitable for where you live. Ask a keen gardener or get advice at a local garden center.

FROM LITTLE ACORNS

In 2007, German schoolkid Felix Finkbeiner wrote a homework report arguing that we all needed to plant more trees. He was asked to read his report at school and word traveled to other schools. Within four years, a tree-planting organization for young people, Plant-for-the-Planet, had been set up. By April 2019, Plant-for-the-Planet had planted a staggering 13.64 billion trees!

Trees grow slowly but surely, so be patient. You could record your tree's progress by taking photos and measurements of it throughout the year.

WILDLIFE WARDEN

The world is teeming with plants and creatures, making Earth an inspiring and fascinating place to live. But Wildlife Wardens are required to help protect the planet's living things.

BIODIVERSITY MATTERS

The extraordinary variety of living things on Earth is called "biodiversity." It is very important to the well-being of the planet because the huge range of species allows healthy ecosystems (see pages 12–13) to thrive. A single ecosystem may contain thousands of different living things, each with their own small role to play.

The different species all help to keep an ecosystem balanced and provide humans and other creatures with homes, food, and essential materials. Yet, all over the world, biodiversity is under threat.

Greater biodiversity makes an ecosystem stronger and more able to cope with changes to its environment.

HOW MANY SPECIES OF LIVING THINGS CAN YOU NAME?

Scientists have classified around 1.75 million species of living things, and new creatures are being discovered all the time:

- There are more than 5,400 species of mammals.

- More than 900,000 insect types have been identified.

- Over 10,900 bird species exist, from hefty ostriches to lightweight hummingbirds.

- A staggering 102,248 species of arachnids—a class of creature that includes spiders and scorpions—have been discovered.

- Scientists have identified 10,793 reptile species.

- There's an incredible 268,000 species of flowering plants.

- Think ferns all look the same? Think again! So far, some 10,500 species have been discovered.

Did you know that a single teaspoon of soil can contain 10,000 to 50,000 different species of bacteria?

UNDER THREAT

Earth's a big, biodiverse place, but human demand for space and resources has caused a catastrophic drop in the population of some plants and creatures. Many species are now endangered or facing extinction. The World Wildlife Fund believes that populations of living things dropped on average by half between 1970 and 2012.

Once the most common bird in America, the passenger pigeon was hunted to extinction by humans. The last bird, Martha, died in a zoo in 1914.

GONE FOREVER

Animals that have recently been declared extinct or are feared to be extinct include:

GOLDEN TOAD

This Costa Rican toad was declared extinct in 2004 (it was last seen in 1989). The cause of its decline is thought to be a combination of deforestation, climate change, and disease.

BAIJI RIVER DOLPHIN

Overfishing, pollution, and deaths by collisions with ship propellers and fishing tackle caused this species of dolphin to rapidly decline. The last confirmed sighting was in 2002 and scientists believe it may now be extinct.

CARIBBEAN MONK SEAL

Once widespread throughout the Caribbean Sea, this seal was hunted to extinction by humans. Overfishing of its food source also contributed to its decline. It was declared extinct in 1994.

NORTHERN WHITE RHINO

The last male, called Sudan, died in 2018, leaving just two females. The species' decline was largely due to humans killing the creature just for the horn on its snout.

MOST AT RISK

The International Union for Conservation of Nature (IUCN) produces a Red List of the most threatened living things. It contains more than 25,000 plant and animal species.

- The white-collared kite is just one of 164 different species of birds threatened with extinction in Brazil.

- In Russia and China, there are thought to be fewer than 100 Amur leopards left.

- There are now thought to be less than 1,000 mountain pygmy possums alive in Australia.

- Less than 500 Mediterranean monk seals now live off the coasts of Turkey and Greece.

- The world's rarest sea mammal is a type of porpoise called a vaquita. Only 30 remain in the waters off California's coast.

- More than three-quarters of all Eastern lowland gorillas in Africa have died out since 1990, leaving under 4,000 of these magnificent beasts.

LOSING THEIR HOMES

Habitat loss is the number one threat to wildlife.
From rainforests to wetlands, natural habitats
are destroyed every day in people's quest
for land, food, and other resources.

URBAN SPRAWL

According to the United Nations, around
4.2 billion people now live in towns and
cities—over five times more than in 1950. As
new towns are built and existing ones get
bigger, they take over land and resources
that were used by other living things.

SPLITTING UP

The demand for food means that ranches
get bigger and break up wild regions. This
creates problems for creatures like big cats
and grazing animals that require huge
territories. As a result, many can't find
enough food or are killed when they stray
into areas where people live and farm.

WETLAND WOES

Wetlands are regions where water meets land,
such as marshes and river deltas. They support
lots of plants and creatures. Many wetlands
have been destroyed to create land for homes,
factories, or farms. In the past 120 years, two-
thirds of the world's wetlands have disappeared.

DAM-NATION

Dams often flood an area of land to form a reservoir. Apart from this direct loss of habitat, dams can also stop fish migrating along rivers. Dead plants that would normally be washed downstream can build up behind a dam, too. As the plants rot, they use up the water's oxygen, meaning the reservoir is unable to support life.

TREE HOUSES

According to the World Wildlife Fund, 30,000 square mi. of forests are cut down each year, causing the creatures who live in them to lose their homes. In Brazil, deforestation has resulted in the number of species threatened with extinction tripling in 15 years. More than 600 species are now at serious risk of dying out.

HABITAT DEGRADATION

Some habitats are not completely taken over by people but are still damaged by their activities. Dredging a harbor to make it deeper, for example, can cause great harm. Dredgers scour the seabed, killing plants and creatures and smothering plenty more with silt and mud.

WILD CRIME

The illegal trade in exotic pets and animal parts is a major threat to some of the world's most endangered species. It can also lead to the introduction of invasive species and diseases.

PETS AND POACHING

Many creatures are protected by law, yet sadly, that does not stop criminals from hunting or capturing them. The illegal wildlife trade is BIG business—the UN Environment Programme estimates it is worth around US$23 billion a year. But what does it actually involve?

Some wild creatures are captured to sell as exotic pets. Often poorly cared for, these animals tend to live miserable, short lives.

Ivory forms the teeth or tusks of walruses, whales, and elephants. The tragic trade in elephant ivory saw African elephant numbers drop by 100,000 between 2010 and 2012 alone. It is estimated that 55 African elephants are still killed every day for their ivory tusks.

Other creatures are killed for their fur, feathers, or skin. Chinchillas were almost hunted to extinction for their soft fur because it took around 150 to make a single coat.

Traditional medicines in some regions of the world call for ingredients made from the body parts of endangered wild creatures, such as tigers, jaguars, and rhinos.

INVADERS

The introduction of invasive species—plants and creatures brought into habitats where they don't belong—can also unbalance ecosystems, especially when the invader starts to breed rapidly. In the past, rats in ships sailed by explorers destroyed entire island populations of seabirds, eating them and their eggs.

Invasive plants can also be destructive. Kudzu is a vine from Asia that now covers more than 300 square mi. in the United States. The vine grows a foot a day, smothering and killing other plants in its path.

In the 1930s, 2,400 South American cane toads were released in Australia to control crop-eating beetles. There are now over 200 million, all covered with a toxic slime that kills many Australian animals.

WHAT CAN YOU DO?

The illegal trade in wildlife and the impact of invasive species is shocking, but there are things you can do to help.

- Stop family and friends from buying exotic animals. Choose pets native to your region or adopt from a rescue center.

- Never release aquarium fish or exotic pets into the wild.

- Never buy items made from ivory, fur, teeth from protected species or sea turtle shells.

- If you suspect someone or a store is selling illegal creatures, ask an adult to investigate and potentially report it.

- Sign petitions to support campaigns against wildlife crime.

CAMPAIGNS AND CONSERVATION

It's not all bad news for the natural world, as many people are working hard to preserve the planet's plants and creatures. The work of conservationists takes many forms, from tracking rare species to rebuilding habitats.

USE YOUR VOICE

Never think that you and your friends are powerless. Public pressure can make a big difference. In 2016, over 500,000 people signed a petition that convinced the European Union to continue to protect many of Europe's wild areas, including wetlands and meadows. And, after years of campaigns, in 2017 the Chinese government banned the buying and selling of elephant ivory. China used to import more ivory than any other nation, so this is a massive step forward.

Some critically endangered species, like this Mauritius kestrel chick, are bred in zoos before being reintroduced into the wild.

In 1974, there were just four Mauritius kestrels left in the world. Following a breeding program and careful protection in the wild, there are now around 400 birds.

IN RESERVE

The world's first large-scale nature reserve was Yellowstone National Park, which opened in Wyoming in 1872. Today, there are over 200,000 of these important places. The UN estimates that they cover 15.4% of the land and 3.4% of the oceans on Earth. Park rangers work hard to protect the environment and creatures in the reserves from poachers, pollution, and illegal dumping.

TAKE ACTION

Join a conservation charity or support its causes by visiting its website, reading about its work, and adding your name to petitions.

Adopt an animal. Many zoos and conservation organizations, including the World Wildlife Fund, Defenders of Wildlife, and Oceana, run schemes that let you contribute to vital conservation work. Why not organize a bake sale at school to adopt an endangered creature for your class?

Visit local nature reserves and see the work performed by rangers. You might even get the chance to volunteer and help out in some way.

BEE ALERT

Bees are not only beautiful creatures, they are also incredibly important to nature and human life. But their numbers are falling all around the world—fast. Bees need your help!

WHAT DO BEES DO?

Bees carry pollen on their legs and bodies as they buzz from flower to flower looking for nectar to eat. Pollen needs to be taken from one flower to another for plants to reproduce. Bees help to pollinate more than 100 important (and tasty) crop species, including beans, apples, and blueberries. Without them, we'd be seriously short of food.

WHY ARE BEES IN DANGER?

Habitat loss and the use of pesticides are two of the reasons bees are struggling. The UK, for example, has lost 97% of its flower-rich meadows since the 1930s. Paving over flower beds and lawns also puts pressure on bees. They simply can't find enough food to eat.

Some bees carry pollen in "baskets" on their hind legs.

NASTY NEONICS

In farming, pesticides called neonicotinoids (neonics) poison the sap and nectar of plants to kill the insect "pests" that try to feed on them. Unfortunately, the casualties include bees and butterflies.

A GUARDIAN GUIDE TO BEING BEE FRIENDLY

The good news is that there's plenty of easy, everyday things you can do to give bees a helping hand. Look at websites of environmental organizations like Friends of the Earth—you can get Bee Saver kits from them and join online campaigns to ban neonics. Why not make your garden, backyard, or window box more bee friendly, too?

- Get your parents to check they don't use plant sprays that contain neonicotinoids.

- Grow plants that flower in winter and spring—times when it can be hard for bees to find food. Check online or at the library to see which plants flower when in your area.

- Plant lupins, lavender, foxgloves, and other bee-friendly plants in flower beds.

- Herbs like marjoram, chives, and rosemary are all easy to grow in pots and good for bees. So are strawberries and raspberries.

- Leave out a shallow bowl or saucer of water for thirsty bees. Bees can't swim, so add some stones or marbles for them to take a drink.

It takes honeybees around two million visits to flowers to make a single pound of honey.

GO WILD

Why not lend bees and other creatures in your neighborhood a hand? Here are a few easy ways to turn an ordinary backyard or schoolyard into a heavenly home for wildlife.

A pile of rotting wood can make an epic home for grubs and small critters. In turn, these can provide food for birds and amphibians.

An old bowl filled with water makes a great mini pond for frogs, insects, and birds. Add a layer of gravel at the bottom of the bowl and some large stones to give creatures ways in and out. Aquatic plants will also keep the water healthy and attract wildlife.

Buy a ready-made bee hotel from a garden center, or build your own following instructions on environmental websites, such as Friends of the Earth. Securely position the hotel at least 3 feet above the ground in full sunlight. Solitary bees should lay their eggs in the tubes, usually sealing them with mud or plant matter.

Leave a patch of grass in your yard uncut. You could plant some wildflower seeds in the patch to create a mini meadow for butterflies, moths, and insects.

Rake up a pile of leaves in fall and leave them undisturbed throughout the winter. This will provide a cozy sanctuary for insects, centipedes, and even little hibernating creatures.

119

GRUB'S UP!

Putting out food for wildlife is a great way to support creatures in your local area. Each region of the world is likely to attract different animals, so do some research about where you live. What sorts of creatures are likely to visit, and what do they like to eat?

FEEDING TIPS

Follow these tips to make sure you're feeding furry and feathered friends the right stuff:

- Don't place bird feeders too close to windows as birds could injure themselves if they accidentally fly into the glass.

- Never feed wild creatures junk food or put out salted or dry-roasted peanuts for birds. Buy raw peanuts from pet shops or garden centers instead.

- If your yard has fruit trees, leave some fallen fruit on the ground. Bruised, rotting fruit provides welcome food for many creatures.

- If you have a bird bath or other supply of water in your yard, keep the water clean. In winter, break any ice that forms over the surface.

120

FEEDING BUTTERFLIES

Butterflies drink nectar from flowers, but will eat sugary liquids from fruit. You can also make sugar water for them, served in a saucer. Just get an adult to boil some rainwater and mix it with several teaspoons of white sugar. Let it cool completely before serving to the butterflies.

Leave some small pieces of overripe fruit outside on a tray for butterflies to have a feast.

FEED THE BIRDS

Bird cake is a mixture of fat, seeds, and nuts that can give a much-needed energy boost to birds, especially in winter. And it's really easy to make your own!

Leave a block of lard at room temperature for a few hours to soften, then cut it into small pieces. Mix it in a bowl with birdseed, raw peanuts, and raisins. Work the mixture together with your fingers until it holds together. You can finish the cake in several ways before placing it in the fridge for an hour to harden:

1. Form it into tight, round fat balls that can sit on a bird table.

2. Make a hole in an old plastic yogurt container and thread string through the hole, securing it with a knot. Pack the pot with cake mix, and once it hardens, hang the pot from a branch.

3. Pack the mix into half a coconut (or you could also use scooped-out orange halves). Get an adult to make a hole in the coconut shell to thread string through, so it can be hung outside.

121

WELL DONE!

You are now a Guardian of the Planet.

But the challenge doesn't stop here. Throughout this book, you've learned how you can help and protect our incredible world. Spread the word to your friends, neighbors, classmates, and family members and encourage them to become Guardians of the Planet, too. If we work together now, we really can make a difference and preserve the planet for generations to come.

If you've been inspired by this book, you might also want to discover a bit more about who ClientEarth are and what they do. Read on to find out more.

A Note from ClientEarth

ClientEarth is a charity that uses the power of the law to protect the planet and the people who live on it. We are lawyers and environmental experts who are fighting against climate change and to protect nature and the environment. We defend forests, oceans, and wildlife. We protect people's health from pollution.

At the moment, our planet is in trouble. We need to act now to make sure the future is a green one for children today—and for future generations. We believe that the law is the most effective tool we have to protect our planet and bring about powerful and lasting change.

By buying this book, you have already supported our work to change the world. But there is so much more we need to do, and we need your help. Find out how you can get involved:

W www.clientearth.org

🐦 @ClientEarth

f @ClientEarth

GUARDIAN GLOSSARY

acid rain
Rain, snow, and fog containing harmful chemicals created by burning fossil fuels.

atmosphere
The collection of gases that surround Earth.

biodegrade
When a substance decays and breaks down naturally.

biodiversity
The variety of living things found on Earth.

carbon dioxide
Colorless gas formed when creatures breathe out and when fossil fuels and other substances are burned. It is a major component of greenhouse gases.

climate
The weather conditions of a region or the entire Earth over a long time.

compost
Plant matter that has decayed naturally and can be used to fertilize soil.

deforestation
The cutting down of large numbers of trees for fuel, timber, or land.

disposable
Something that is thrown away after it is used.

dredge
To clear materials from a river, lake, or seabed.

ecology
The study of relationships between different living things and their environment.

ecosystem
A collection of all living things and their nonliving surroundings in one particular area.

endangered
Used to describe a species of living thing that is threatened with the possibility of dying out.

enhanced greenhouse effect
The buildup of carbon dioxide, methane and other gases in the atmosphere, trapping more of the Sun's heat and affecting the climate.

evaporation
The transformation of water from liquid to gas.

extinction
When a species of living thing dies out and no more of its number exist.

fossil fuels
A natural fuel formed in the Earth from the ancient remains of animals and plants, such as coal and oil. Fossil fuels contain high amounts of carbon, which is released when they are burned.

generators
Devices that are powered to create electricity.

geothermal energy
Heat energy taken from underneath the Earth's surface.

global warming
The warming up of the Earth's surface due to changes in the gases that form the Earth's atmosphere.

greenhouse gases
Gases in the atmosphere, such as carbon dioxide, methane, water vapor, and nitrous oxide, which trap heat from the Sun and warm the Earth.

habitat
The surroundings that a particular species needs to survive. Habitats include coral reefs, grasslands, lakes, and deserts. Some creatures live in more than one habitat.

incinerators
Devices used to burn solid waste at garbage dumps.

kilowatt-hour (kWh)
A measure of energy used by many electricity companies. It is equal to the energy expended by 1,000 watts in an hour.

microplastics
Extremely small pieces of plastic, millions of which get into rivers, lakes, and oceans where they can be harmful to marine life.

ozone
A colorless gas, a layer of which exists in the Earth's atmosphere and protects the planet's surface from the Sun's harmful rays.

pesticides
Poisonous substances that kill animal or insect pests.

photosynthesis
The process in which a plant uses energy from sunlight to produce food for itself.

poaching
The catching and killing of wild creatures for profit.

pollen
Very fine grains that plants produce and use to create new plants.

pollution
Waste products or heat that damage the environment in some way.

recycling
The process of turning old waste materials, such as paper and glass, into something new.

renewable energy
Energy from a source that can be restored and maintained. Wind and solar power are both examples of renewable energies.

resources
Natural things found on Earth, such as metals, trees, coal, or water, which can be used in some way.

sap
Liquid that travels around a tree or other plant to keep it healthy.

species
A group of animals or plants that are similar and can mate to produce offspring.

sustainable
Able to continue over a long period of time with little or no harm to the environment.

ton
A measurement of weight, equal to 2,000 pounds or 907 kilograms.

UN
Short for United Nations—the international organization that encourages people and countries to work together peacefully and for the benefit of all.

vegan
A person who not only does not eat meat or fish (as a vegetarian does), but also does not eat or use any animal products including milk, cheese, honey, and eggs.

INDEX